Institute of Leadership
& Management

superseries

Managing the Effective Use of Equipment

FIFTH EDITION

Published for the
Institute of Leadership & Management

ELSEVIER

AMSTERDAM • BOSTON • HEIDELBERG • LONDON • NEW YORK • OXFORD
PARIS • SAN DIEGO • SAN FRANCISCO • SINGAPORE • SYDNEY • TOKYO
Pergamon Flexible Learning is an imprint of Elsevier

Pergamon
Flexible
Learning

Pergamon Flexible Learning is an imprint of Elsevier
Linacre House, Jordan Hill, Oxford OX2 8DP, UK
30 Corporate Drive, Suite 400, Burlington, MA 01803, USA

First edition 1986
Second edition 1991
Third edition 1997
Fourth edition 2003
Fifth edition 2007

Editor: David Pardey

Based on material in previous editions of this work

The views expressed in this work are those of the authors and do
not necessarily reflect those of the Institute of Leadership &
Management or of the publisher

Notice
No responsibility is assumed by the publisher for any injury and/or damage to persons or
property as a matter of products liability, negligence or otherwise, or from any use or operation
of any methods, products, instructions or ideas contained in the material herein

British Library Cataloguing in Publication Data
A catalogue record for this book is available from the British Library

Library of Congress Cataloguing in Publication Data
A catalogue record for this book is available from the Library of Congress

ISBN 978-0-08-046432-9

For information on all Pergamon Flexible Learning publications
visit our website at http://books.elsevier.com

Institute of Leadership & Management
Registered Office
1 Giltspur Street
London
EC1A 9DD
Telephone: 020 7294 2470
www.i-l-m.com
ILM is part of the City & Guilds Group

Typeset by Charon Tec Ltd (A Macmillan Company), Chennai, India
www.charontec.com
Printed and bound in Great Britain

07 08 09 10 11   10 9 8 7 6 5 4 3 2 1

Contents

Contents

Series preface

Whether you are a tutor/trainer or studying management development to further your career, Super Series provides an exciting and flexible resource to help you to achieve your goals. The fifth edition is completely new and up-to-date, and has been structured to perfectly match the Institute of Leadership & Management (ILM)'s new unit-based qualifications for first line managers. It also harmonizes with the 2004 national occupational standards in management and leadership, providing an invaluable resource for S/NVQs at Level 3 in Management.

Super Series is equally valuable for anyone tutoring or studying any management programmes at this level, whether leading to a qualification or not. Individual workbooks also support short programmes, which may be recognized by ILM as Endorsed or Development Awards, or provide the ideal way to undertake CPD activities.

For learners, coping with all the pressures of today's world, Super Series offers you the flexibility to study at your own pace to fit around your professional and other commitments. You don't need a PC or to attend classes at a specific time – choose when and where to study to suit yourself! And you will always have the complete workbook as a quick reference just when you need it.

For tutors/trainers, Super Series provides an invaluable guide to what needs to be covered, and in what depth. It also allows learners who miss occasional sessions to 'catch up' by dipping into the series.

Super Series provides unrivalled support for all those involved in first line management and supervision.

Unit specification

Title:	Managing the effective use of equipment	Unit Ref:	M3.29
Level:	3		
Credit value:	1		

Learning outcomes	Assessment criteria		
The learner will	*The learner can (in an organization with which the learner is familiar)*		
1. Understand the need for effective and efficient use of equipment	2.1 Explain why equipment should be used effectively and efficiently 2.2 Describe how the use of equipment is monitored and controlled in the workplace 2.3 Explain why it is important to have a scheduled maintenance programme for equipment in the workplace 2.4 Compile a simple maintenance programme for equipment in the workplace 2.5 Conduct a simple risk assessment of equipment security in the workplace, and explain how these risks could be reduced		

Workbook introduction

1 ILM Super Series study links

This workbook addresses the issues of *Managing the Effective Use of Equipment*. Should you wish to extend your study to other Super Series workbooks covering related or different subject areas, you will find a comprehensive list at the back of this book.

2 Links to ILM qualifications

This workbook relates to the learning outcomes of Unit M3.29 Managing the effective use of equipment from the ILM Level 3 Award, Certificate and Diploma in First Line Management.

3 Links to S/NVQs in management

This workbook relates to the following Unit of the Management Standards which are used in S/NVQs in Management, as well as a range of other S/NVQs:

D6. Allocate and monitor the progress and quality of work in your area of responsibility.

4 Workbook objectives

In 1995 Sir John Harvey-Jones wrote:

> We talk continuously about the need to improve our productivity and, God knows, it is a dire need: yet we appear to accept with equanimity that in the world of work we are achieving less than half our capacity. Luckily for us few other countries do much better, but the potential for improvement is so vast that it is incomprehensible that we do not debate, study and struggle to do better.
> (Source: John Harvey-Jones (1995) *All Together Now*, Mandarin.)

What was true in 1995 is, sadly, still true today. We still have a long way to go before we can say that our businesses run as efficiently as they might.

However, by deciding to study this workbook you have taken the first step towards addressing the problem of managing your organization's resources in an efficient and secure manner.

There are three sessions. Sessions A and B deal with ways of measuring and analysing work processes: productivity, work study and some of the latest thinking about how to improve the efficiency of organizations.

> A story which illustrates the distinction between efficiency and effectiveness is that of a surgeon who was said to have improved his efficiency by completing more operations in a day, only to reduce his effectiveness as all his patients died.

All organizations would like their employees to be more efficient because **efficiency** is normally equated with profitability. One way of expressing efficiency is as an equation: what you get out divided by what you put in:

$$\frac{\text{What you get out}}{\text{what you put in}}$$

Effectiveness, on the other hand, has to do with how good you are at achieving what you set out to achieve.

One misplaced fear is that increased efficiency leads to job losses. The argument is that fewer people will be needed to perform the same tasks. In fact, the opposite is generally true. When efficiency goes up, an organization becomes more prosperous, is able to expand its sphere of activities, and so more people are likely to be needed. However, with appropriate security, this prosperity can easily be diminished. In session C we look at steps that can be taken to ensure a secure workplace.

4.1 Objectives

When you have completed this workbook you will be better able to:

- identify and use some method study techniques to help you improve efficiency and effectiveness;
- plan for the best use of resources, including people, assigned to you;
- contribute effectively to the control of your organization's resources;
- play your part in helping to improve the efficiency of your work team and your organization;
- identify risks to the security of resources and have gained some practical ideas and experience with which to guard against them.

5 Activity planner

The following activities require some planning so you may want to look at these now.

- Activity 8 on page 27 starts the process of creating a structured approach to increasing efficiency by finding ways to advance the potential of your team. This is continued in Activity 14 on page 34.

- Activity 9 on page 28 helps you to make optimum use of your workspace. You might like to start making a note of problems and requirements now. This is continued in Activity 15 on page 35.

- Activity 10 on page 29 will provide you with the basis of a structured approach to increased efficiency in the use of machinery and equipment. This is continued in Activity 16 on page 36.

- Activity 11 on page 30 provides the basis of a structured approach to increased efficiency in the use of materials. This is continued in Activity 17 on page 37.

■ Activity 13 on page 32 provides the basis of a structured approach to improving the use you make of sources of information. This is continued in Activity 19 on page 40.

■ Activity 18 on page 38 provides the basis for a structured approach to making better use of energy in the workplace.

Some or all of these Activities may provide the basis of evidence for your S/NVQ portfolio. All Portfolio Activities and the Work-based assignment are signposted with this icon.

The icon states the elements to which the Portfolio Activities and Work-based assignment relate.

The Work-based assignment (on page 68) asks you to develop one pair of these Activities into a complete plan for improving efficiency with respect to one resource at your command. This could also be used to form the basis for your portfolio of evidence. You may want to prepare for it in advance.

Session A
Productivity and work study

1 Introduction

We know what efficiency is, but how can we measure it? How will we recognize it when we see it?

If possible, it would be useful to express efficiency in numerical terms, so that we have a sound basis for comparison. And if we were able to divide work activities into small elements, we could set a standard time for performing each one, and calculate how long a task 'should' take, compared with what it does take.

The techniques described in this session attempt to do these things. Productivity reduces efficiency to a simple ratio. Method study is the breaking down of tasks into individual elements, and then analysing them. Work measurement uses techniques to determine how long a qualified worker takes to do a specified job to a defined level of performance.

2 Productivity

If you recall, our definition of efficiency was as follows:

Efficiency means making the best use of resources to achieve production of goods or services.

In its simplest form, efficiency can be expressed as a ratio of what we get out for what we put in, i.e.:

$$\frac{\text{output}}{\text{input}}$$

This ratio is referred to as **productivity**, and can be applied at a national as well as organizational level.

Let's put some numbers into this ratio. Say the inputs – the resources used – for a certain job cost £1000 and the output was valued at £2000.

Then the input: output ratio would be:

$$\frac{2000}{1000}$$

We can simplify this to:

$$\frac{2}{1}$$

This is known as the job's productivity ratio.

If we wanted to get an increase in productivity we could either **increase** the output for the same input or **decrease** the input for the same output. If for example we could increase the output value from £2000 to £3000, the ratio would become:

$$\frac{3}{1}$$

On the other hand, if the resource input costs fell from £1000 to £500 (with the output still valued at £2000), the ratio would become:

$$\frac{2}{0.5} \text{ or } \frac{4}{1}$$

In other words:

Productivity rises if the output is increased without increasing the input, or if the output stays the same but the input is decreased.

2.1 Company productivity ratios

Some examples of productivity ratios used in organizations are:

(a)
$$\frac{\text{Sales}}{\text{Labour hours}}$$

(b)
$$\frac{\text{Sales}}{\text{Pay}}$$

(c)
$$\frac{\text{Value of shipments}}{\text{Labour and materials}}$$

(d)
$$\frac{\text{Value of production}}{\text{Cost of labour} + \text{materials} + \text{capital} + \text{overheads}}$$

Activity 1

3 mins

Consider the following example.

Suppose you own a vineyard, and have the aim of getting rich by making lots of high quality wine. You could measure your productivity as:

1
$$\frac{\text{Number of bottles of wine produced}}{\text{Number of hectares of vineyard}}$$

2
$$\frac{\text{Value of wine produced}}{\text{Labour costs}}$$

3
$$\frac{\text{Value of wine produced}}{\text{Cost of all resources used}}$$

(a) Which ratio would give you the best overall indication of efficiency? Tick your answer.

1 ☐   2 ☐   3 ☐

(b) Are all these ratios true measures of efficiency? Circle your answer.

Yes/No

Explain your answer to question (b):

_____

_____

Perhaps you will agree that ratio 3 is the best overall indication of efficiency. But what about the answer to (b)?

Suppose now that in one year in your vineyard you have a good crop of grapes, but make a mistake and pick them at the wrong time. You would probably still be able to make large quantities of wine, but it wouldn't be very good. You might have to sell the wine at a price that barely made you a profit.

If you used ratio I, you could claim that your productivity was high, in terms of yield per hectare. This is a perfectly valid measure of productivity, and is the kind of figure used to compare the output of one vineyard with another. However, if you picked your crop at the wrong time you can hardly profess to have made 'the best use of resources', so your efficiency cannot be said to be high. (Incidentally, your effectiveness would not be very good, either, as you will have failed in your aims.)

Often, ratios and other statistical information can be misleading, and it is important to think carefully about what the figures really mean. In the above case, the key difference was that ratio I was in terms of the number of bottles, not the wine's value. In commercial organizations, it is sensible to assess over-all productivity as a ratio of money: cost and value.

3 Cost benefit analysis

To achieve efficient and effective working we have already established that there will be associated costs. We have also considered the different types of resource needed to support an organization's activity. Associated with each of the four types of resource – people, capital, materials, information – there are bound to be costs. Costs can fall into two types:

- quantitative
- qualitative.

'Quantitative' is the term used when costs are described in numerical terms or units. For example, if we state that the cost of an item was £23, we are using the quantitative description. 'Qualitative' is the term used when costs are set out in broad descriptive or less tangible terms. For example, if we state that the cost to the business was a decrease in morale, we are using the qualitative description, i.e. it is difficult to attribute numerical terms in this instance, but there is a cost nonetheless.

The same terms and terminology can be attributed to benefits.

We can use cost benefit analysis methodology in a range of instances, for example:

- when purchasing a new piece of equipment
- when introducing new work schedules
- when changing staff rostering systems.

A cost benefit analysis is likely to result in some form of business case in order to justify a decision (positive or negative) that is being made. This case may be made formally in report format, in a presentation, or simply during discussions with others within the organisation.

3.1 Costs

EXTENSION 1
For more detail on managing costs, see *Operations Management* by Howard Barnett.

To justify the purchase of a new piece of equipment, or any form of change, it is generally accepted that the total benefits will exceed the total costs.

If, for example, you have been asked to conduct a cost benefit analysis in relation to the potential purchase of a new piece of capital equipment, costs will possibly include:

1 The investigation of possible suppliers, including calls, travel and time.

2 The actual purchase (or lease if this is an option).

3 Installation and commissioning of the equipment.

4 Delivery and location on-site.

5 Time spent training staff on how to use.

6 Duplicate costs incurred in running of existing equipment during phasing-in stage.

7 Down time if old equipment is to be removed before installation of new.

8 Staff down time while waiting for installation.

9 Potential opportunity costs where, if the money is spent on one thing, the opportunity is lost for spending it on something else.

Activity 2

Which of the above costs are quantitative and which are qualitative?

Quantitative:

_____

_____

_____

Qualitative:

_____

_____

_____

The answers to this question can be found on page 80.

3.2 Benefits

Benefits are always likely to have associated timescales; they may be immediate benefits or they may become apparent in the short-, medium- or long term.

Benefits may be:

- actual reduction in costs
- saving time, for example where old equipment requires a high level of maintenance and/or repair
- saving physical effort, for example where new equipment is designed in a way which reduces the physical energy required to operate more efficiently and effectively
- transfer of labour to other areas
- more skilled workforce that can adapt more readily to future technological advances.

These benefits will be in quantitative and qualitative terms, and it may not be easy to specify the actual long-term benefits to the business as a whole, particularly where they are clearly qualitative benefits.

The remainder of this session will explore the examination of work methods, or work study, as it is more commonly known. Cost benefit analysis will always be important here, as it will be necessary to decide where changes in work methods are required, and what the costs and benefits of these changes might be.

4 Work study

4.1 Introduction to work study

Earlier, you read about ways of expressing and measuring productivity. We've established that you increase productivity by becoming more efficient. But how do you become more efficient?

Often, though not always, this involves examining work methods. Doing this might lead you to change the way the workplace is laid out, change the sequence in which things are done, change an administrative system so you can make better use of computer power and so on. The systematic examination of work methods is called **work study** – we are going to look at work study now.

The following sections will only provide a brief introduction to this rather specialized subject; they will:

■ give you a taster of what work study tools and techniques are available
■ provide you with some insight into the methods used by a specialist department or by outside consultants.

4.2 What is work study?

EXTENSIONS 2 AND 3
The books listed in these extensions at the end of this workbook will enable you to find out more about work study.

In most kinds of jobs efficiency depends (at least partly) on the methods used to do the work. **Work study** aims to analyse work methods and the materials and equipment used in order to:

■ determine the most economical way of doing the work
■ standardize the method, and install it as standard practice
■ establish the time required by a qualified and trained worker to carry out the job, at a defined level of performance.

Work study has two distinct but related aspects: **method study** and **work measurement**. The following diagram gives definitions of method study and work measurement, and shows how they are used together to improve productivity and efficiency.

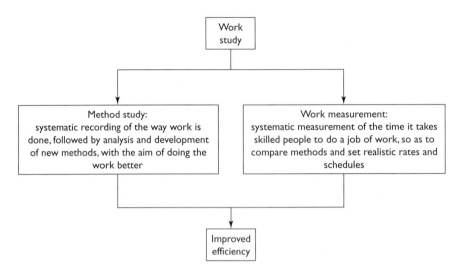

5 Method study

Essentially, method study involves breaking a job down into individual elements, and then analysing them. By probing and questioning, we hope to eliminate ineffective and inefficient methods and procedures and replace them with better ones.

There are six steps to method study. These are likely to overlap, but it is important that each step is completed in the sequence shown in the diagram below:

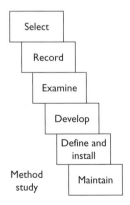

These steps can be remembered by the initial letters of the words: SREDDIM (**S**heep **r**arely **e**at **d**ead **d**aisies **i**n **M**ay).

The steps should help you:

- focus on the problem you're trying to solve
- write down your findings, so you can consider them more easily
- not to jump to conclusions
- decide what action you're going to take
- make sure your new method works, and keeps on working.

The next few pages contain a brief explanation of each of these six steps.

5.1 Select

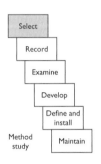

This stage is concerned with systematically examining and selecting a specific problem that needs to be solved, or an area of work that needs to be studied. The key things that must be taken into account are:

- potential savings
- investigation costs
- the extent of the resulting project – its scope and required outcomes
- the length of time that it will take to complete the project.

In selecting a problem or area the four main considerations are:

- **financial**, the impact on the organization's finances
- **technical**, where the solution is itself of a technical nature, or where the introduction of new technology forces changes in work methods to be made
- **human**, where there will be likely changes in working practices which will impact on the people concerned
- **environmental**, i.e. the impact on the local and/or wider environment.

5.2 Record

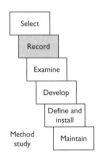

A systematic approach to method study requires systematic recording techniques. These techniques will support the person carrying out the method study in:

- recording all the relevant facts in a standardized way
- developing a clear illustration of what is happening.

Five activities have been identified which can be used to describe work activities of many kinds; each has been assigned a special symbol. The symbols are shown in the chart below.

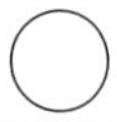	**Operation**:	(Remember 'O' for operation.)
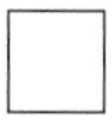	**Inspection**:	(Think of looking at something through a square window.)
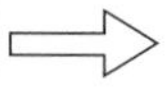	**Transport**:	(The arrow suggests movement.)
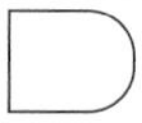	**Delay**:	(Looks like a 'D' for delay.)
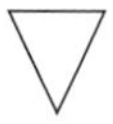	**Storage**:	(Imagine a cone-shaped storage container.)

There are variations on these symbols, but the ones above are the most commonly used and understood.

Consultants and work study experts use a variety of recording techniques. These include:

- **flow process diagrams** – these diagrams are drawn onto a scale diagram of the actual work area
- **string diagrams** – pins are inserted onto a scale plan of the working area. These pins will indicate nodes where, for example, work activity takes place and delays occur. Lengths of thread are used, tied between the relevant pins, to show the exact route of the work process – the total length of the thread used, in relation to the scale diagram, will be used to indicate distance materials travel, movement of people, information, etc.
- **multiple activity charts** – these are used when a team works together on any one work process. The chart will record individual team member activity in relation to a common timescale.

There are also other variations on these recording methods, and of course computer packages exist that can produce diagrammatic illustrations of these types, based on data that has been input.

5.3 Examine

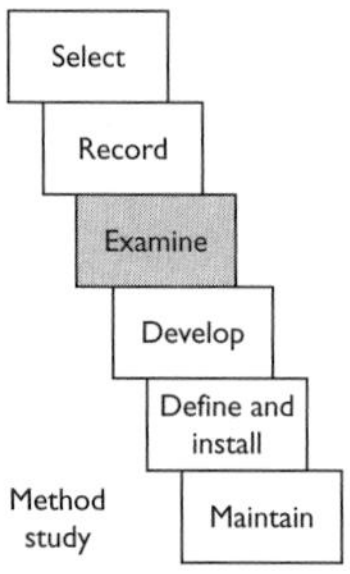

The examination stage starts with a number of telling questions. By questioning, you hope to establish:

- the facts as they are
- the underlying reasons
- the alternatives
- the means by which things can be improved.

There are many questions you might ask, including:

- 'What is the purpose of the activity?'
- 'Why is it done in this location?'
- 'Why is it done by these particular people?'
- 'Why is it done in this time period?'

We can usefully categorize these questions by separating them into two sets, which we can call **primary questions** and **secondary questions.**

Primary questions concern current methods, and should relate to the following five headings:

- **purpose**: What is accomplished? Why is it necessary?
- **means**: How is it done? Why in this way?
- **place**: Where is it done? Why here?
- **sequence**: When is it done? Why at this time?
- **person**: Who does it? Why this person?

The purpose of the secondary questions is to try to propose alternative methods and to select the best of these alternatives. The options are first listed:

- What **alternative purposes** are there?
- What **alternative means** are there?
- What **alternative places** are there?
- What **alternative sequences** are there?
- What **alternative people** are there?

Then the best of these alternatives is chosen.

5.4 Development

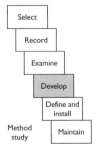

The secondary questions trigger the development stage, which will result in a new method being selected from the proposed alternatives.

Improvement to an existing work process could be brought about by, for instance:

- eliminating a redundant activity
- modifying an activity
- combining two or more activities
- changing the location of the work
- altering the sequence of activities
- simplifying the means of doing the work.

5.5 Define and install

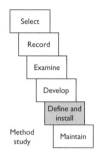

Select

Record

Examine

Develop

Define and install

Maintain

Method study

When the investigation has been completed, it is necessary to describe the proposed new work method in detail. This is to enable:

■ the method to be installed
■ training and instruction to be given
■ a reference to be provided, in case of any disputes or misunderstandings, and when further changes are being considered.

Anyone investigating a problem or work area should have consulted the people involved at every stage. Installation will certainly be made more difficult if the full co-operation of those affected is not obtained.

Often it is simply not possible to switch suddenly and completely from one method of working to another.

Activity 3 · 10 mins

You have investigated the Goods Receiving processes in place across the 23 very busy depots of your organization. It has been run as a manual system since the company was established in 1973, but your recommendation to computerize these processes has been accepted, and you have been given the go-ahead to organize purchase of the relevant hardware, software and installation of this at each of the depots.

What are three of the problems you would now have to plan to deal with?

_____

_____

_____

Your problems might include:

■ how to run parallel electronic and manual systems, and for how long
■ how training can happen, and how everyone concerned will receive the training without major disruption to the operation of each depot
■ organizing the work area to allow the computer equipment to be installed

- issues of health and safety in terms of location of equipment
- implementation of relevant health and safety regulatory requirements that will affect individual staff members.

Installing a new method, system or procedure may require a great deal of planning. This stage should really be considered very early on in the project, if the difficulties are to be overcome easily.

5.6 Maintain

Once the new method is installed and is working properly, suitable controls should be introduced to ensure that:

- new problems are overcome as they arise
- improvements are maintained
- a regular system of feedback is established to monitor performance, targets and quality
- appropriate modifications are introduced to deal with changing conditions
- necessary paperwork actually aids the new method and does not hinder it.

Activity 4 · 4 mins

Perhaps you will agree that, over a period of time, agreed procedures and practices tend to be altered. From your experience of controlling work activities, what are the reasons why people tend to move away from prescribed methods? Try to list **two** reasons.

_____

_____

_____

_____

_____

_____

You may agree that people tend to alter their ways of doing things, whether consciously or unconsciously, because:

■ the agreed method does not achieve the results required. For example, a procedure that says: 'Cut the 5 metre pipe into 4 equal lengths of 1.25 metres,' might be impractical because it doesn't allow for the material lost during the cutting operation
■ the method may make the job rather awkward or tedious. Most people will tend to do work in the way that is most comfortable for them
■ circumstances change, so that the method needs to be modified.

Maintaining an installed method means making sure:

■ the method actually works in the way you think it does
■ the people involved are happy and comfortable with the method
■ the method is modified, in a controlled fashion, to deal with changing conditions
■ that management or those who commissioned or sanctioned the study are happy that the project objectives have been met.

That completes our review of method study techniques. Now we move on to the other aspect of work study: work measurement.

6 Work measurement

Imagine the following situation.

You have started up a factory making emergency and first-aid packs. You started off in quite a small way but have become fairly successful, and are now taking on a number of new staff.

You have to keep your costs to a minimum, as you have very little to play with in the pricing of your products. Some of your problems are that:

■ you want to pay your employees a bonus for meeting production targets, but don't know at what rate these bonuses should be set
■ you need to know what your costs are very precisely, including the time taken to carry out each task in the manufacturing process
■ you need to know how many product items can be produced each week

■ some method study investigations have been carried out, resulting in proposals for new methods of working; you now need to be able to compare these new methods with existing ones.

Managers are frequently faced with problems like these. To run a business – or any other kind of organization – successfully, it is seldom good enough to rely on broad-brush estimates: precise information is needed.

This is where work measurement can be useful.

EXTENSION 1
Operations Management
by Howard Barnett
includes a chapter on
measuring work
content.

Work measurement is defined as the use of techniques to establish how long it takes a qualified worker to do a specified job to a defined level of performance.

Work measurement enables **standards** to be set so that:

■ different methods for doing a job can be compared
■ work can be organized so as to achieve optimum results using the available resources
■ incentive schemes can be reasonable and fair
■ defined cost levels can be established
■ realistic planning and estimating can be done for the future.

Work measurement is a well-established technique for providing precise information about the length of time to do a job. It is an important aid in increasing efficiency because it enables management to make accurate calculations, and enables proposed new methods to be compared.

In undertaking any form of work measurement the business will be seeking to identify and introduce methods for improving process efficiency. A range of work measurement techniques is available, with new and improved techniques being introduced all the time. Common forms include variations of:

■ time study
■ activity sampling.

6.1 Time study

This is probably the best known and most widely used technique. It involves the recording of the times and rates of working for clearly identified short elements of a job, usually by direct observation. A stopwatch or an electronic timing device is used.

The stages of time study are as follows.

1 Select the job to be studied

   Ideally, **method study** should have already been applied to the job. There's no point in measuring work which is known to use inefficient procedures.

2 Break down the job into short parts or phases called **elements**

   Elements are short distinct tasks (such as tightening a screw, or moving an item from one location to another). It is important that each element is separately recognizable. Normally jobs are broken down into elements which take no more than half a minute to complete.

3 Record the activity to obtain the **observed time** for each element

   There are several difficulties attached to observation, not the least of which is that people tend to behave differently when they are being watched.

4 Calculate the **standard time** for the job

6.2 Activity sampling

Suppose the management of an organization want to find out the percentage of time spent on each of a number of activities. One obvious way to ascertain this information would be to set up time studies to observe the activities of each person or machine continuously over a period of time. For a large organization the cost of such an exercise would be very high indeed.

An alternative for this – and for other situations where it isn't practicable to spend large amounts of time and effort on continuous observation – is to take **sample** observations.

If, for example, a machine is being used intermittently, one approach to activity sampling would be to:

1 Observe the use of the machine over a defined period, for example one day.

2 Record the pattern of use, i.e. show when the machine is in use and when it is not in use.

3 Calculate the amount of time the machine has actually been in use. This is done by the following method:

$$\frac{\text{number of idle segments}}{\text{total number of segments}} \times 100$$

4   Carry out further observations at random points over a defined period of time, for example every fourth day in a fortnight.

This sampling approach will not give exact results, but should offer a reasonable picture of what is happening, and provide some basis for decision making.

Activity 5

Briefly identify two advantages and two disadvantages of time study and activity sampling.

_____

_____

Advantages of time study and activity sampling are:

■   an analytical approach to particular aspects of work
■   a quantitative measurement, with quantitative outcomes
■   if undertaken by external experts, a means of gathering objective and impartial information.

Disadvantages include:

■   potentially complex types of information which is not readily understood by everyone
■   statistical results of activity sampling may not be based on a relevant time period
■   it separates the process from the people carrying out the process, which may result in individuals feeling alienated from resulting recommendations.

6.3 Improving process efficiency

Increasingly the emphasis has shifted from analysis of processes to the implementation of more pro-active approaches to improving overall process efficiency. Organizations have been able to compare their performance with that of their competitors, whilst encouraging staff to make suggestions on potential improvements that can be made. Continuous improvement is recognized as a more effective means of embedding change where suggestions for improvement have been made by those who are most affected by the change. This is also a far more cost-effective approach to improvement, as it can happen as and when required, in relevant and practical stages.

▪ 7 Calculating staffing requirements

Productivity is dependent to a great extent upon having the staff available to do the job required. As a team leader you will be aware of how important it is to make sure that you have enough staff available to carry out the work, and that these staff need to have the necessary skills to work effectively. A business needs to do likewise, but on a wider and longer-term basis. Human resource planning, as it is known, is concerned with forecasting what position the business will be in the future – where its markets will be, what those markets will want – and calculating how to meet those needs in human resource terms.

The need for replacement or additional staff will arise for a number of reasons.

Activity 6 · 4 mins

List some of the reasons for replacing or adding new staff.

_____

_____

_____

_____

_____

_____

The reasons will include:

- changes in working practices
- staff leaving through retirement, career progression, and so on
- introduction of new technology
- increase in productivity requirements.

Productivity and quality can be negatively affected where human resource forecasting is not carried out on an ongoing basis. Think of how your area would cope if a key member of staff were to leave unexpectedly. Productivity could drop where other staff members had to step in to carry out their colleague's work, and quality could be affected too, because others may not fully understand what quality requirements are in place for that particular job role. At the same time, if staff are having to carry out more work than normal their own work levels and work quality may suffer.

You need to be constantly aware of how productivity and quality are affected by changes in staffing.

To support this human resource planning process you need to know and understand the different factors that affect your own work area. These factors are:

- numbers of staff needed to carry out current work requirements
- skills and knowledge levels required to carry out these work requirements, possibly in the form of job specifications for each role within the department or team
- potential changes to work requirements, based on information gathered
- organizational, departmental and team objectives
- number and types of staff required to fulfil these objectives.

This information is likely to be recorded in a variety of ways, with some of it being contained in staff records. You may hold this information yourself, or it may be located elsewhere. Records will need to reflect further details on team members, including:

- specific skills and knowledge of each individual in relation to work requirements
- specialist expertise – for example, first aid certificate, fork lift truck licence
- training programmes completed
- evaluation of performance – for example appraisal, performance review records
- career goals.

Activity 7

20 mins

What information do you have on your team members that can support the human resource planning process?

_____

_____

_____

_____

With this information it is possible to adapt quickly in the event of a staff member unexpectedly leaving your team. As a team leader you can consider what is required, examine the capabilities of the staff you have available, identify gaps in provision and identify where a new staff member may be required.

Using reliable and valid human resource information in the face of changes to work and work requirements will facilitate the decision-making processes and help to ensure that productivity and quality can quickly return to required levels.

Self-assessment 1

20 mins

1 The inputs to a process cost £2500, and the outputs are valued at £4500. Five people are employed on the process. Work out the overall productivity, and the output per head.

2 Insert the correct words from the list below

(a) _____ is the term used when costs are described in numerical terms or units. _____ is the term used when costs are set out in broad descriptive or less tangible terms.

(b) To justify the purchase of a new piece of equipment, or any form of change it is generally accepted that the total _____ will exceed the total costs.

(c) In undertaking any form of _____ the business will be seeking to identify and introduce methods for improving process efficiency.

(d) In the second stage of time study you will break down the job into phases called _____.

STAGES	WORK MEASUREMENT
CHARGES	BENEFITS
QUALITATIVE	CONSULTANCY
ELEMENTS	QUANTITATIVE

3 The steps of method study have become muddled up in this diagram. Put them in the correct order.

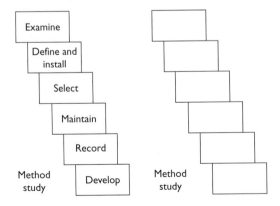

Examine
Define and install
Select
Maintain
Record
Method study
Develop
Method study

4   What are the four main considerations, in method study, when selecting a specific problem, a problem that needs solving or an area of work that needs to be studied.

_____

_____

_____

_____

5   Identify two factors that affect managers in their own working area, in relation to human resource planning.

_____

_____

Answers to these questions can be found on pages 78–9.

8 Summary

- Productivity is expressed as a ratio of what we get out for what we put in, i.e.

$$\frac{\text{output}}{\text{input}}$$

  Productivity rises if the output is increased without increasing the input, or if the output stays the same but the input is decreased.

- Cost benefit analysis methodology can be used in a range of instances, often to justify a business case.

- Work study, comprising method study and work measurement, aims to analyse work methods, and the materials and equipment used, in order to:

  - determine the most economical way of doing the work
  - standardize the method, and install it as standard practice
  - establish the time required by a qualified and trained worker to carry out the job, at a defined level of performance.

- Method study is the systematic recording of the way work is done, followed by analysis and development of the new methods, with the aim of doing the work better.

- Work measurement is the systematic measurement of the time it takes a skilled person to do a job of work, so as to compare methods and set realistic rates and schedules.

- Method study consists of the following steps:

  1 Select the problem or work area to be studied.
  2 Record what is actually taking place at the moment.
  3 Examine and analyse what has been recorded and find out any inefficiencies or shortcomings in existing methods.
  4 Develop alternatives to existing methods which are both new and improved.
  5 Define and install the new method(s).
  6 Maintain the newly installed method(s), to make sure they have achieved the required level of efficiency.

- Method study recording techniques include process charts, flow process diagrams, string diagrams and multiple activity charts.

- In undertaking any form of work measurement the business will be seeking to identify and introduce methods for improving process efficiency. A range of work measurement techniques is available, including time study and activity sampling.

- Increasingly the emphasis has shifted from analysis of processes to the implementation of more pro-active approaches to improving overall process efficiency.

■ Continuous improvement is recognized as a more effective means of embedding change.

■ Human resource planning is concerned with forecasting:

  ■ where the business will be in the future
  ■ where the markets will be
  ■ what those markets will want
  ■ how to meet those needs in human resource terms.

■ Productivity and quality can be negatively affected where human resource forecasting is not carried out on an ongoing basis.

Session B
Efficiency in your workplace

 ## 1 Introduction

You should note that, although this session is shorter than the last, it contains a number of Activities which may involve you in several hours of work.

Terry Wisham, the Chief Executive of Clairbuoys Ltd, attended a presentation by one of his managers on the application of work study techniques to some of the organization's methods. He listened with interest, but gave a guarded response.

'OK. Supposing we spend several weeks of valuable time recording and measuring,' he said, 'working out exactly how long it should take to perform these tasks, what then? What I'm interested in is in finding efficiency improvements that are real and lasting.'

These techniques, which you read about in the last session, are useful and interesting. However, they are not magic formulae which will lead to efficiency enhancements automatically. They are practical tools which are intended to be used with careful thought and planning. If and when you do apply them, it may not be entirely apparent how they will help you in your search for increased efficiency. So what's the best approach?

You will recall that we noted in Session A that **it is in the management of resources that the key to efficiency lies**. It is therefore the aim of this next session to help you identify:

- the resources you have
- ways of planning for saving on these resources.

2 What are the real costs of using resources?

We know that maintaining and improving efficiency consists of making the best use of available resources. Now it's time for you to answer the question:

> In relation to your own job and circumstances, how do you plan to 'make the best use of available resources'?

All resources have costs associated with them – the cost of purchase, the cost of use, the cost of maintenance, the cost of update or replacement, the cost of not using the resource efficiently and effectively. All organizations need to understand that a resource which is not used as it should be is a wasted resource, and as such has associated costs. In Session B we considered cost benefit analysis and so you will understand the type of costs we need to take into account.

To maximize resource efficiency a business needs to understand what resources actually cost. As a manager you need to know and understand the costs of:

■ running an item of equipment
■ an item of equipment lying idle
■ running a faulty, poorly maintained item of equipment
■ staff
■ replacing staff
■ producing items, and the marginal costs of producing just one more item than is required.

This is not a complete list and you can probably identify further costs that will affect the efficiency of the workplace.

First, you will need to identify the resources at your disposal.

Let's look at each type of resource in turn.

2.1 People

People are a special kind of resource. It could be said that they are the most difficult resource to develop and, if badly handled, may bring the downfall of the organization. On the other hand, if you get your team fully motivated and working towards the right objectives, efficiency and effectiveness will follow almost automatically.

Activity 8

S/NVQ D6

This Activity, together with a later one (Activity 14 on page 34), will provide you with a basis for a structured approach to increasing efficiency, by finding ways to advance the potential of your team.

This Activity may provide the basis of appropriate evidence for your S/NVQ portfolio. Whether or not you decide to do this, you may like to use these two Activities as a basis for a plan of your own; you can come back to them periodically when you are thinking about possible improvements in efficiency.

Use a separate sheet of paper for this Activity.

Write down the names and brief details of your team members. If you feel you know an individual reasonably well, just jot down in brief notes his or her main skills and experience. (Remember, this is for your own benefit, and no one else's.) If you find this difficult, it may be that you need to find out more about the person concerned; in this case, remind yourself of the fact.

Then try to think of at least one kind of task that you think each person is capable of performing, that he or she does not currently do.

Set out your sheet of paper as follows, repeated for as many people as you have in your team.

Name and main job function	Brief summary of skills and experience
	I need to get to know more about this team member ☐
This person has the potential to:	

2.2 Workspace

We listed land and buildings among the main resources of organizations, but when it gets down to individual teams it is more appropriate to talk about workspace.

Activity 9

10+ mins

S/NVQ
D6

This Activity, together with a later one (Activity 15 on page 35), is designed to help you to make optimum use of your workspace.

This Activity may provide the basis of appropriate evidence for your S/NVQ portfolio.

Your next task is to study the workspace which you are able to use.

It may be appropriate to draw a plan, if your team all work in one area. Alternatively, you could just make a list. Remember that your eventual aim is to find better ways of using your workspace.

(For some managers, for example those who lead teams who are travelling most of the time, or who spend their time on other organizations' premises, this Activity may not be very meaningful. If this is the case with you, ignore it.)

2.3 Machinery and equipment

When we consider machinery and equipment we generally have to take into account a variety of items, ranging from simple tools to complex machinery. Simple tools tend to be reliable, and at the same time they do not require costly maintenance, however, they do still have to be available to support the work that needs to be done. Machinery and more complex equipment may form the essential foundation of a key work process, for example computerized telephone systems in call centres – without these the purpose of the business cannot be fulfilled.

The purpose of the next Activity is to identify essential equipment and machinery in your work area, then to consider the use of each item, as well as any problems encountered.

Activity 10

S/NVQ D6

This Activity, together with a later one (Activity 16 on page 36) will provide you with a basis for a structured approach to increased efficiency in the use of machinery and equipment.

This Activity may provide the basis of appropriate evidence for your S/NVQ portfolio.

Use a separate sheet of paper for this Activity.

Compile a list of all the essential equipment and machinery within your area of work. The items that you identify must be essential to the overall fulfilment of the purpose of your work area, that is, without the item the work could not continue and objectives could not be achieved.

For each item ask the following questions:

■ What is it used for?
■ Who uses it?
■ How frequently is the item used?
■ How easy is it to use (how much training and support)?
■ What problems have we had with this item over the past week, month, quarter?
■ How quickly was the problem resolved?
■ What maintenance (in terms of frequency and complexity) is required?

To make this Activity more effective you might want to involve your team members in compiling the list and in answering the questions.

2.4 Materials and components

Now we come to the things that get used up in the transformation process.

Activity 11

15+ mins

S/NVQ
D6

This Activity, together with a later one (Activity 17 on page 37), will provide you with a basis for a structured approach to increased efficiency in the use of materials.

This Activity may provide the basis of appropriate evidence for your S/NVQ portfolio.

Identify the materials and components that are the inputs to your team's work process, together with any consumables.

This time, it might be relevant to also note down your current wastage rate for each item, if you know it. (There may be a number of reasons why wastage occurs, apart from spoiled material. For example, a team servicing computers will need to carry parts, some of which may become outdated before they are used.)

Again, make the list as detailed as you feel is appropriate for your needs. If you are able to write down this list without reference to other sources, a quick summary may be all that's required. But if you are not clear about what kinds of materials are used by your workteam, it could be a good idea to do some research on the subject.

Use a separate sheet of paper as before.

2.5 Energy

The amount of energy your team uses can be measured by your fuel utilization. The difficulty with identifying this resource is that, typically, electricity and other forms of fuel will be shared with others in the organization. It is more productive to discuss ways of saving energy, and we'll leave discussion of this resource until later in the session.

2.6 Time

Time is allocated to everyone equally, and yet is still very precious. Perhaps it is not a good idea to ask you to identify how much time you have to spare, as you may decide to leave the paper blank!

2.7 Finance

The amount of financial responsibility given to team leaders and first line managers varies considerably. For the next Activity, you are asked to write down the extent of your own authority to handle finances.

Activity 12

5 mins

How much scope do you have when it comes to spending the organization's money?

(a) How large a budget do you control, if any, and what kind of items are you permitted to buy or hire?

_____

_____

_____

(b) If you do not have your own budget, how much practical, effective control do you have over the purchase of materials, the hiring of people, etc.? (For example, you may not officially be a signatory on documents that authorize the spending of money, but your recommendations may, to some extent, be accepted without question.)

_____

_____

_____

(c) To what degree do you feel your efforts are being frustrated by the lack of control you have over finances? Do you think you could make your team more efficient if you were able to make more financial decisions, for example? If so, how could you persuade your manager of this?

_____

_____

_____

2.8 Information

This is the last item on our list of resources. Sources and types of information are many and varied, and are therefore difficult to summarize. Instead, you are asked to identify deficiencies.

Activity 13

15+ mins

S/NVQ
D6

This Activity, together with a later one (Activity 19 on page 40), will provide you with a basis for a structured approach to increasing efficiency by improving your sources of information.

This Activity may provide the basis of appropriate evidence for your S/NVQ portfolio. If you are intending to take this course of action, it might be better to write your answers on separate sheets of paper.

What kinds of additional information, if any, would help you and your team do your job more efficiently? Answer the following questions by encircling your response and explaining it briefly.

(a) Would you or your team work more efficiently if you were given more information about the processes or procedures you work with?   Yes/No

Explain: _____

_____

_____

(b) Would you or your team work more efficiently if you were given more information about the activities of other teams or other parts of the organization?   Yes/No

Explain: _____

_____

_____

(c) Is there any other kind of information that would help to make you or your team work more efficiently?   Yes/No

Explain: _____

_____

_____

3 Planning for improved efficiency and effectiveness

Now that you have spent some time analysing and identifying the resources that are currently available to you, it is time to start making plans to:

- utilize those resources in a better way
- obtain additional resources that would help to make you or your team more efficient
- increase your effectiveness.

This section looks at how to maximize the use of available resources. This will involve planning and evaluation, and building, on the information which you produced in completing the Activities in section 2.

Plans will need to take into account the costs associated with the required actions, but at the same time demonstrable benefits should result from taking the planned actions.

3.1 People

There are many approaches to the management task of getting the best from people. Here are a few ideas to add to your own.

- Training

Often, individuals feel frustrated at not being able to carry out their work as efficiently and effectively as they would like, because they have not been fully trained. Training may consist of specific instructions and guidance regarding a particular process or procedure, such as how to operate a machine, how to use some computer software, or the safest method of evacuating a building. These are the technical skills.

Your team may also require training in financial, administrative or interpersonal skills.

But remember, too, that the training needs of your team may have more to do with their lack of understanding of the principles, or the rationale behind the work they are asked to do, than the development of specific skills.

Thinking people want to know more than **how** to do something, they need to know **why**. For example:

- cooks and chefs need to understand the concepts behind nutrition, as well as cooking methods and recipes
- accountants in a manufacturing company will do a better job if they have a good appreciation of the processes they are being asked to cost
- health club instructors may improve their performance if they are trained to explain the effects of particular exercises on the body, rather than simply showing visitors how to use gym equipment.

Training sessions do not need to be expensive, although it is important that they are conducted in a professional manner.

- Coaching

  A coach is someone who aims to get the best out of people: the best efforts, the best achievements, the best ideas.

  By coaching you can:

  - convey the objectives of the organization and the team, so that everyone works to the same ends and in the same direction
  - create an atmosphere in which the team is encouraged to work out its own solutions to problems, through understanding, not by simply following a rigid set of steps
  - get people to believe in themselves, and their ability to improve their efficiency and effectiveness.

- Empowering and delegating

  The modern concept of a manager is primarily as leader – someone who sets out to gain trust, influence and commitment, and is prepared to give respect and power to the team.

  It is the team who must get the job done, and it is the leader's role to provide them with the means to do it: to empower them.

  Virtually any and every task can be delegated.

Activity 14 · 15+ mins

S/NVQ
D6

This Activity, together with Activity 8 on page 27, will provide you with a basis for a structured approach to increasing efficiency, by finding ways to advance the potential of your team.

This Activity may provide the basis of appropriate evidence for your S/NVQ portfolio.

In Activity 8, you were asked to make notes about the members of your team. Now you should use your response to decide what actions to take in order to get the best from these resources. Use the following questions to help you make your decisions. Write your answers on separate sheets of paper.

(a) What training will you arrange for each of your team members, that will help them to become more efficient or effective? Skills training (technical, administrative, financial, interpersonal)? Education, to give greater awareness and understanding?

(b) How will you start coaching people to achieve their objectives, and to believe in themselves and their ability to solve their own problems?

(c) How do you intend to delegate more tasks, and to empower the team to achieve more?

3.2 Workspace

Badly used workspace can result in:

- **congestion** – if workstations are too close together, for example

- **accidents** – if there is not enough room, corridors aren't clearly marked, or gangways are blocked

- **inefficient communications** – when people can't see each other, when there is too much noise, or when too many people have to use the same phone

- **excessive energy costs** – when doors and windows are left open, or a building is badly insulated

- **low production** – if there are breaks and discontinuities in the flow.

Activity 15

S/NVQ
D6

This Activity, together with Activity 9 on page 28, is designed to help you to make optimum use of your workspace.

This Activity may provide the basis of appropriate evidence for your S/NVQ portfolio.

In Activity 9, you set out the workspace available to your team. In doing so, you may have thought up some ideas of the ways in which you might improve the use of the available space, or some means of acquiring additional space.

Now set up a meeting with your team about this subject. What problems do they see? How would they solve them? (You may be able to delegate this whole task, and take on the role of coach and facilitator.)

Write down the results of your meeting on a separate sheet of paper, and say what your next step will be.

3.3 Machinery and equipment

Earlier (in Activity 10), you were asked to list the essential equipment and machinery your team uses, and to identify any problems with it. Now's the time to think about ways of solving those problems, and of utilizing these items more efficiently.

Activity 16

30+ mins

S/NVQ
D6

This Activity will provide you with a basis for a structured approach to making better use of your work equipment.

This Activity may provide the basis of appropriate evidence for your S/NVQ portfolio.

Consultation with your team will help to establish practical and supported approaches to using machinery and equipment more effectively and efficiently.

Review the information gathered in Activity 10, focusing in particular on the following questions.

■ How long is the item left idle – and why?
■ What maintenance-related problems have we experienced?
■ What other common problems have arisen regularly?

Reflect on the results from this analysis. Where possible calculate the costs, qualitative and quantitative, of:

- idle equipment
- maintenance-related problems
- other common problems.

Now build a plan for tackling each of these areas. This plan should show what action is needed, and the estimated costs of such action. You may also wish to produce a formal maintenance schedule where it is clear that maintenance is a core problem with wide-ranging costs. A maintenance schedule can be established which takes account of peak working times, shift patterns and manufacturers' guidance (remember: warranties may only apply where proof of regular maintenance is available). As you have already learned, maintenance will have costs, but the benefits are likely to far outweigh these.

3.4 Materials and components

As already mentioned, there may be a good deal of scope for making savings on materials and components.

Activity 17

15+ mins

S/NVQ
D6

This Activity, together with Activity 11 on page 30, will provide you with a basis for a structured approach to increased efficiency in the use of materials.

This Activity may provide the basis of appropriate evidence for your S/NVQ portfolio.

Following your response to Activity 11, you need now to help the work team find ways of optimizing the use of the materials and components you use. Prompt responses from your work team members by posing the following questions:

(a) How can we reduce wastage of materials and consumables?

(b) Are the materials and components we use the best ones for the job?

(c) If the answer to (b) is no, how can we identify and obtain better ones?

(d) Are the processes we use making the best use of the materials and components?

(e) If the answer to (d) is no, how can the processes be improved?

(f) Are our end products what our customers want?

(g) If the answer to (f) is no, what can we do about it?

3.5 Energy

The key to efficiency when it comes to energy use is simple: save as much of it as possible.

Activity 18 · 10+ mins

S/NVQ
D6

Use the following checklist to help you find ways of saving energy. (The 'you' in this Activity refers to you personally, or any member of your team.) Tick the boxes.

	Yes	No
(a) Do you know how much energy you are using?	☐	☐
(b) If not, can you find out and bring it to the attention of the team, so you can monitor improvements?	☐	☐
(c) Do you take trouble to ensure that heating, lights and machinery are switched off when they aren't needed?	☐	☐
(d) Is there a proper system of maintenance for boilers and other energy-consuming equipment?	☐	☐
(e) Do you keep doors and windows closed during the winter months?	☐	☐
(f) Does the building where you work have efficient heat insulation?	☐	☐
(g) Do you encourage or reward the saving of energy?	☐	☐

Now give your own ideas for saving energy:

_____

_____

_____

_____

_____

_____

Finally, on separate sheets, write down the steps you are going to take to make savings in energy.

3.6 Finances

An overall measure of efficiency, and the one that accountants and chief executives are inclined to use, is the amount of profit made by the organization this year as compared to last. In simple terms, the input is the amount of money put into the enterprise, and the output is the amount of income. The difference is the profit.

The best way to save money is to become more efficient in the use of your resources.

If you are responsible for a budget, you may need to improve your administration and control procedures. You could perhaps:

- keep better records of expenditure and the use of materials, ensuring they are complete, accurate and accessible
- ensure you monitor and maintain resources such as equipment and materials in accordance with organizational requirements
- keep your team members informed of their individual responsibilities for the control of resources
- ensure that, if you need to make spending decisions which thereby exceed your budget, you refer to your line manager or other relevant authority.

3.7 Information

The next (and last) Activity on the efficient use of resources requires you to plan to find the information you and your team need.

Activity 19

S/NVQ
D6

This Activity, together with Activity 13 on page 32, will provide you with a basis for a structured approach to increasing efficiency by improving your sources of information.

This Activity may provide the basis of appropriate evidence for your S/NVQ portfolio.

In Activity 13 you made notes on the kind of information you think you are lacking in. Now explain how you intend to obtain this additional or alternative information.

_____

_____

_____

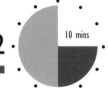

Self-assessment 2

1 Fill in the blanks in the following sentences with suitable words chosen from the list below.

(a) If you get your team fully _____ and working towards the right _____, efficiency and effectiveness will follow almost automatically.

(b) A _____ is someone who aims to get the best out of people: the best _____, the best _____, the best _____.

(c) It is the _____ who must get the job done, and it is the _____'s role to provide them with the means to do it: to _____ them.

(d) Badly used workspace can result in _____, _____, inefficient _____, excessive _____ costs or low _____.

ACCIDENTS   EFFORTS   MOTIVATED

ACHIEVEMENTS   EMPOWER   OBJECTIVES

COACH   ENERGY   PRODUCTION

COMMUNICATIONS IDEAS   TEAM

CONGESTION   LEADER

2   List **four** ways to save energy for someone who works in an office.

_____

_____

_____

_____

3   Make **three** suggestions for controlling finances better, for someone who controls a budget for a small department.

_____

_____

_____

_____

4   Give **three** examples of costs associated with the use of resources.

_____

_____

_____

_____

Answers to these questions can be found on page 79.

4 Summary

This session has mainly consisted of suggestions and Activities designed to help you and your work team become more efficient and effective. Among the questions posed were the following.

■ Do you know and understand the costs of:

- running an item of equipment
- an item of equipment lying idle
- running a faulty, poorly maintained item of equipment
- staff
- replacing staff
- producing items, and producing just one more item than required?

■ Is your use of people efficient and effective? Are they:

- trained to perform their assigned tasks
- enabled to develop their skills
- empowered to take control of their work?

■ Could you delegate more tasks?

■ Are you, the manager, acting as a leader who not only sets out to gain trust, influence and commitment, but is also prepared to give respect and power to the team?

■ How can you utilize your workspace in a more efficient and effective way, so as to avoid:

- congestion
- accidents
- inefficient communications
- excessive energy costs
- low levels of production?

■ How can you improve your management of equipment and machinery? Is there some that:

- is under-utilized
- is in a poor state of repair
- is badly suited for the task it is used for
- you understand the operation of insufficiently?

■ If you are responsible for a budget, how can you improve your administration and control procedures? Could you perhaps:

- keep better records of expenditure and the use of materials, ensuring they are complete, accurate and accessible
- ensure you monitor and maintain resources such as equipment and materials in accordance with organizational requirements

- keep your team members informed of their individual responsibilities for the control of resources
- ensure that, if you need to make spending decisions which thereby exceed your budget, you refer to your line manager or other relevant authority?

■ Would you or your work team work more efficiently if you were given more information about the processes or procedures you work with?

■ Would you or your work team work more efficiently if you were given more information about the activities of other teams or other parts of the organization?

■ Is there any other kind of information that would help to make you or your work team work more efficiently?

Session C
Security in the workplace

1 Introduction

Security for home and family is a basic human aspiration. An attack on home or family, having property stolen and personal financial information rifled and misused are amongst people's worst nightmares. Similar fears haunt the managers of all organizations.

2 Types of security threats

If security fails it can affect employees, who may lose their jobs or even their lives as a result. So it is in *all* employees' interests to help employers create a secure working environment. The theft of physical property or physical harm to 'human resources' are evident from missing goods or injuries. Less obvious, but potentially more 'threatening' to the organization, is the theft of vital information, which is its very lifeblood.

Activity 20

Think of two examples of threats that can arise to the security of each of the following.

1 Physical property

_____

_____

2 People

_____

_____

_____

3 Information or 'data'

_____

_____

When you think about it, you'll discover that there are many possibilities. You may have included some of the following possible threats.

- Theft by customers or employees; attack by other creatures, such as insects, birds, rodents; destruction or damage by fire or flooding.
- Assault by robbers, other staff, or the general public; injury caused by defective buildings or equipment; damage to wellbeing from hazardous substances, fumes, fire or flood.
- 'Poaching' of key employees by competing organizations.
- Industrial espionage – theft of trade secrets; copying of materials; confidential records, e.g. costings; management accounts; personnel records; commercially sensitive information such as discounts allowed to major customers; proposed activities that might affect share prices; the despoiling of information deliberately by the introduction of computer viruses.

The possibilities are infinite and businesses are increasingly vulnerable for some or all of the following reasons.

- The size of manufacturing plants, distribution warehouses and stores increases. The loss of one 'key site' or plant can be ruinous if you've nowhere as large to fall back on.

- The decreasing 'tolerance threshold' of some people makes them a threat to employees in contact with the general public, such as in hospitals, transport/ leisure facilities and shops.
- Information stored (and retrievable) electronically is highly portable and also prone to attack by computer hackers – think how much data can be stored on one floppy disk.

A major fire, the theft of a payroll, or the death of key personnel in a transport accident will have serious consequences. But it is statistically more probable that an organization will suffer the theft of information; or unauthorized use, malicious corruption or destruction of that information. Data held electronically is potentially accessible to **anyone, anywhere** in the world.

Commercial secrets

Over the centuries, organizations have guarded zealously 'trade secrets' such as recipes, industrial processes and trading terms given to customers. For example, some recipes have been handed down through the generations and their knowledge restricted to the fewest possible employees.

But, someone has to have the recipe for a product to be made – and if it is made by computer controlled equipment, the chances are that somewhere it will appear in an electronic memory which will not endure torture unto death to protect it!

Activity 21

3 mins

Picture the following breaches of security and suggest the adverse consequences that might arise for the organization suffering them.

1 the weatherproofing of a third world country grain warehouse is breached by rodents

_____

_____

2 the sales manager of a commercial company is enticed to work for their major competitor

_____

_____

3 the payroll arrangements for distributing wages paid in cash to a multi-site retail company are accessed by a disgruntled former employee

Obviously, the consequences could be very serious in all three events.

This workbook is not mainly concerned with the risks to health and safety, which are dealt with fully in *Managing Health and Safety at Work*.

- At its worst, there could be destruction of grain stocks by the rodents or by fire if they have damaged electrical wiring. That could lead to starvation for people already vulnerable through hunger. Whose responsibility would that be – the rodents or the people managing the grain store?
- The sales manager will have confidential information about trading terms, possibly company production methods and recipes, plus personal contacts and standing with major customers.
- Unauthorized access to payroll data may have helped the competitor make the sales manager an 'offer not to be refused'. This could lead to a major theft, or series of thefts if the employee chooses to share the information with criminals. If the criminals are armed, serious injury or death could result as well as loss of property.

These simple examples show that security lapses don't all come from deliberate theft and that one breach of security can easily lead to another – like a game of Consequences, which is really a light-hearted approach to risk management.

3 Risk management approaches to security

Professional risk management is the best defence against security lapses. It is also used in the health and safety arena, where you may already have encountered it. Below is a five-step approach.

Five-step approach to assessing and minimizing risks to resources

1 **Identify** the resources at risk.
2 **Assess** the **probability** that the risk will be realized.
3 **Evaluate** the consequences.
4 **Prioritize** the consequences.
5 **Implement** a strategy to eliminate or minimize the risks – tackling the worst first.

There is a major difference, however, between safety and security. Safety is concerned with hazard, while security deals with the intrinsic vulnerability of resources.

Hazard

In safety management, hazard is the intrinsic potential of anything to cause harm, such as the capacity of asbestos fibres to cause fatal or serious illness.

In safety risk management, the recommended Health & Safety Executive approach says: *eliminate the hazard and you will eliminate the risk*, e.g. find a way of replacing asbestos with an entirely different material which achieves the same degree of thermal insulation but is not hazardous.

Vulnerability

In security management, hazard becomes the **intrinsic vulnerability** of the resource, for example:

- the direct financial value of materials like diamonds, CDs, alcohol or cigarettes;
- the difficulty of replacing key buildings and equipment;
- the skills, knowledge and 'marketability' of people;
- the worth of data to a competitor or organization you may have to negotiate with.

Intrinsic vulnerability is necessary. You can eliminate hazard, but you can't eliminate intrinsic vulnerability without destroying the organization's ability to function.

If your business is manufacturing industrial diamonds, or CDs, you cannot eliminate them from it. If you did replace the vulnerable resource, the replacement is likely to be as vulnerable as the item it replaces, but you **can** assess the risks to it and follow through the five-step process to eliminate or minimize the risks.

3.1 Using risk management to safeguard personnel; stock; equipment and data

You can apply the five-step approach in two ways: first to each resource individually and secondly for activities where the resources overlap.

You'll be asked to look at each in turn during this session.

The invaluable 'what if' question

Implicit in all risk management is the simple but powerful question 'what if?' It is easy to remember and excellent for assessing the potential consequences of any risk, or series of risks, to all resources.

Look at it applied in several different situations

- 'What if' we open our restaurant after the local pub closes. Is there a risk to our staff from customers who have had too much to drink?
- 'What if' we go over to self service in our shops. Could it increase 'shrinkage' and negate the planned savings in staff wages?
- 'What if' we allow employees to take equipment home to work with. Is there a greater risk of it being damaged or stolen?
- 'What if' there is a fire at our payroll bureau. Do we, and/or they, have back up information available that is right up to date?

You can ask yourself the 'what if' question in any security management situation for two different reasons.

- As a short-cut way of assessing risks before implementing the full five-step analysis.
- As a way of reviewing a security strategy already implemented. It could be that a previously unconsidered potential risk has arisen, or changes to procedures are being considered.

Use the grid provided as Extension 4 to make an assessment of the security risks in the following scenario. Ask yourself the 'what if' question about all aspects of the scenario.

Activity 22

EXTENSION 4
Format for making five-step approach to security risk assessments

A cash and carry warehouse is just extending a branch and has asked you as the responsible manager to conduct a security risk assessment before the work starts. During the three month project, up to 20 contractors' staff will be working on site and will have to gain access via the main staff entrance and existing warehouse. Some overhead work will be involved and, at some stage, the contractors will need to break through the existing external wall, close to some high storage racking. The main computer terminal will have to be moved to a new office. It has been agreed that contractors staff can use company fork lift trucks, provided that they are licensed drivers and obtain formal permission from you on every occasion. Of the 50 company staff on site, around 40 are paid in cash on Thursday afternoons.

At the Glastonbury Festival in 2002, a high security fence was erected around a wide perimeter to prevent 'gatecrashers' entering the event without paying. As this is an open air event in a large space, there is less potential conflict with safety issues than in, for example, an upstairs dance hall.

In the limited time available, make your assessment and indicate the strategy you would use to minimize each risk you identify.

You will find a model solution in the reflect and review session (on page 81).

There is no '100% right' solution in this situation, any more than there is in real life situations you may face at work. So, your solution may differ in some respects from the 'model'. The Activity will have given you some experience of the process of assessing risks and of deciding what the priorities should be for tackling the consequences identified.

3.2 The security versus safety conflict

Although there are similarities in approaches to security and safety, there are also potential conflicts. There can be a real struggle between the need to achieve maximum security and the priority to protect the lives of people who may be inadvertently 'imprisoned' by security measures. Some terrible losses of life have occurred in stores, sports arenas, nightclubs and dance halls, where security devices prevented the victims escaping. It is understandable that owners of premises wish to control access and prevent gatecrashers getting in without paying (this is effectively a form of theft) but it is completely unacceptable, morally or legally, to risk people's lives in the attempt to achieve 100% security.

Often, problems are caused by security bars and locked or blocked emergency exits which prevent people escaping when a fire has started, or when a panic has caused people to stampede towards the exits. When people are shopping, working or sleeping upstairs, as in a department store, hospital or hotel, they are especially vulnerable.

Minimizing the risks to personnel and visitors

There can be no greater risk to the security of personnel and visitors than finding themselves on the third floor, with the fire exits and windows securely barred in front of them as the spreading smoke and flames begin to overtake them.

Simple, but effective safeguards for all upstairs rooms demand that:

■ there are at least two safe ways out, which are well separated and not dependent on lifts that cannot be used in emergencies;
■ all emergency exits can be opened rapidly from the inside and are kept clear of obstructions on the outside.

...

3.3 Common sense security

A labourer on a building site was challenged several times by a security guard as he passed through the gate pushing wheelbarrow loads. All the contents of the barrow proved to be worthless and bore out his claim that he was taking rubble to an off-site skip. It transpired that he had stolen ten wheelbarrows. This frequently told story does illustrate how simple strategies often defeat security systems.

The five-step risk management approach is a well proven, professional means of assuring security. However, it should not prevent you looking for simple, common sense ways to protect property against theft.

Look at the following case study, based on real events

Example

A heavy goods vehicle driver, wearing an overall displaying a company logo, walked up to a fork lift driver in the despatch warehouse of a large company. He said he couldn't find anyone on the loading bay to load his vehicle and would they please help. At the bay, he indicated the largest of the assembled palletized loads – some ten tonnes of material, which they helped him to load. He thanked them politely for their help, secured his load and drove off, never to be seen again.

The driver arrived when most people, including the area's team leader, were on their lunch-break. He spoke politely and confidently to the staff and appeared to be in no hurry. There was a security gate, but it wasn't the only way out of the site. The load he took was worth several thousand pounds.

Very often, the simplest strategies are the most effective for a thief. Looking confident, appearing to know the way around and even asking for help can be much simpler, safer and more profitable than using dynamite, tunnels or guns. Such simple methods may even gain the thief grudging admiration for impudence and audacity.

But it affects the profitability of the business and, if repeated often enough, the security of employees' jobs can be jeopardized.

Activity 23 · 5 mins

Think about your own working area from a security perspective. Imagine that you are a potential thief on the lookout for easy pickings and think what you might be able to steal.

It will help you to use two of the concepts already introduced in this session.

1   *Vulnerability* – which items are most vulnerable to theft, through high value and portability? Remember to look at tools and raw materials that you use, as well as stocks of finished goods.

2   *What if* – ask yourself this question over matters such as changes of personnel; changes in working methods; storage facilities; suppliers; siting of entrances and exits; goods receipt and despatch systems – anything which could affect the security of materials, especially the most vulnerable to theft.

Draw up a list of priorities for discussion with your boss.

> When you have decided on your priorities, be careful with whom you discuss them and where you put the list. Just in case any weaknesses you identify come to the knowledge of the 'wrong' people.

Restricting access

Preventing people from entering areas where they do not need to be almost certainly figured in your list and in the arrangements for your own workplace.

It makes sense to classify areas into **low, medium, high** and **restricted categories**, with increasingly stringent access requirements including passes, passwords and keys, swipe cards or security guards for the highest categories.

However, there are many organizations that find this approach difficult to implement fully. Hospitals, shops and shopping centres, leisure facilities, hotels, restaurants, airports, railway stations, amongst others, cannot bar the general public from many areas and indeed invite them to come in. For example, if you are going to see a relative in hospital, you will not wish to go through draconian security procedures taking 20 minutes to complete, yet the hospital will have large amounts of vulnerable materials including drugs on its site.

Even in the most secure sites where there is no public access, security systems in place have been designed by the 'wit of man' and so can be unravelled by the 'wit of man'. Locks, bars, photo cells and all the technical devices may achieve nothing if the local area supervisor doesn't challenge an official looking visitor who seems unfamiliar, or a security guard whose face is unknown.

Careless talk

There was a famous World War Two poster which showed a scene in a pub, or some other place where people had the chance to chat to one another. Above the scene it said simply:

'CARELESS TALK COSTS LIVES.'

Large numbers of people – including yourself – need access to information that is confidential. It may be vital to you doing the job, but it could lead to breaches of security if seen or heard by the wrong people.

Here are some examples of information made freely available to outsiders, by employees who did not ask themselves: 'What is the security risk if this got into the wrong hands?'

Example

'We always take the money to the bank at 3 pm. If we don't, there's hell to pay from the retail manager.' (Shop manageress, talking to distribution driver whom she had kept waiting.)

'The payroll van comes along at 4 o'clock on a Wednesday afternoon, regular as clockwork.' (Wages office, talking to stranger complaining about access to site.)

'The safety officer insisted we removed the bars from that office window. He said we must find a safer way, though we've not found one yet' (heard in local pub, near to large store).

'It's not been announced yet, but that site will be closing next month, so we're re-routing all the vehicles ready for when it happens.' (Distribution depot – talking about customer's site where more than 200 jobs would be lost.)

Security risks from written documents – paper and electronic

Computer screens often display confidential information about personnel, costings, payroll and financial matters to anyone who cares to read them. This happens in open plan offices and even in reception areas where the receptionist doubles as a clerical employee. Receptionists may also then have to discuss confidential matters over the internal phone system within earshot of visitors. The extensive use of faxes and emails increases the availability of information. An envelope marked 'confidential' or 'to be opened by addressee only' at least creates a physical barrier and anyone who reads it without authorization knows they could be in trouble, whereas a fax coming through in a general office may be read by anyone, and an email circulated without need to a dozen people may end up giving information to dozens more, just like a chain letter.

Here are some real examples of security breaches from written documents.

Example

An engineering company made an unauthorized video of reconditioned equipment installed on a manufacturing site. No-one on the shop floor challenged them, as they were so used to seeing engineers from the company around. The video included shots of a monitor screen displaying a secret recipe. (The engineers, to be fair, did not realize its significance.) They used the video for marketing purposes and the recipe was seen by a rival manufacturer who was also buying from the same engineers. It was no longer a secret!

The personnel director of a company employing tens of thousands of people was horrified to find that a union official with whom he was negotiating knew his final offer position to the fraction of a penny. He surmised later that the national negotiator was adept at reading writing upside down and had read it from his notes. That cost his company dearly at the year's wages settlement. The following year, he relied on his memory!

A major company was rumoured strongly to be planning a move from London to a town 20 miles away, certainly entailing many redundancies. The rumours were hotly denied. Then, a headline appeared in the financial press, giving full details of the move. The information was accurate. It transpired that an estate agent dealing with the acquisition was married to someone who worked in public relations for the company that was moving and had warned the spouse – who had let it slip to a contact on the newspaper which then published the story.

None of these real life examples involved any complicated technology or code cracking ability. Preventing them required only the use of basic common sense security approaches and personal integrity – costing nothing. But they cost the organizations involved dearly in terms of both cash and embarrassment.

The 'need to know' principle

This commonly applied security principle says simply that information should be provided to people on the basis that they 'need to know' it in order to do their job. In hierarchical terms, the 'higher' you climb up the management ladder, the more information you probably need to know.

Directors normally have access to all or most information, but even here, data such as discount levels to major customers, may be restricted.

Does the production director 'need to know' what override discounts are given, or the sales director the tentative 'final offer' decided on for this year's wages review? Probably not, and the fewer people who know, the less chance is there that they will tell anyone else, deliberately or accidentally.

In reality, many people at *all* levels in the hierarchy 'need to know' a great deal of confidential information and, ultimately, have to behave in a trustworthy fashion. This creates potential problems in open plan areas, including those in offices, banks, building societies and shops.

Activity 24

5 mins

Underline the confidential information which each occupation in the following list probably 'needs to know' to do the job. Be strict in your interpretation.

1   Wages and salaries clerk:
    cash payroll delivery arrangements; basic salary and commission rates for sales staff; details of forthcoming pay offer.

2   Sales representative:
    annual override discounts for major customers; details of most profitable lines to sell; credit ratings for each customer.

3   Mixing machine operator:
    recipes for specialist products; costs of all ingredients used; total costs of producing lines for which mixes are provided.

4   Checkout sales assistant:
    details of promotional offers; gross margins on all lines sold; arrangements for banking cash at local branch.

5   Team leader for the distribution planning department:
    wages costs for delivery driver; profit margins on each product distributed; fuel costs of using different types of vehicle.

You will probably have come very close to the model answer, though you might disagree on some points.

1   A wages and salaries clerk probably needs to know only basic salary and commission rates for sales staff.

2   A sales representative probably needs to know details of 'most profitable' lines to sell and credit ratings for each customer.

3   A mixing machine operator probably needs to know recipes for specialist products and costs of all ingredients used.

4   A checkout sales assistant probably needs to know only details of promotional offers.

5   A team leader for the distribution planning department probably needs to know only the fuel costs of using different types of vehicle.

The need for integrity

Most people enjoy the feeling that they know something which others don't – 'knowledge is power' is an oft repeated truism. It is also true that many people enjoy 'letting slip' some of the knowledge which they have, for whatever reason. This is where many breaches of security arise.

■ In the example of the company moving its office, the breach occurred when one spouse warned the other that their job might be at risk. This happened even though the information imparted was supposed to be completely confidential to the estate agency and senior staff in the company for whom they were acting.

It is easy to let slip information in social situations and it is often difficult to know where the communications line will end. It can move like a geometric progression where:

1 A tells B something – so now two people know.

2 B tells C and D – so now four people know.

3 C and D each tell two other people (E, F and G, H) – so now eight people know.

4 E, F, G and H each tell two other people – so now 16 people know.

The 'confidential' information will soon spread to dozens more. Whether or not that matters depends on what those people do with it, apart from telling other people.

But, the more people who know something sensitive, such as confidential plans for major changes to an organization, the more likely it becomes that it will be used in a way which harms the organization and the interests of both it and its employees.

Your team will look to you for an example in this area of management and will respect you more if you don't breach the confidence you have been trusted with.

3.4 Insurance

It is often believed that damage to property, or theft of stock, or damage to equipment, doesn't matter that much because 'the insurer will pay up'. This is wrong, for a number of reasons.

The iceberg principle

Just like an iceberg, many aspects of a loss insured against are below the surface. While the direct costs of replacing a wrecked asset or stolen goods may be covered, many others below the surface are not, typically:

- loss of productive time;
- loss of morale – especially where injuries have occurred;
- diversion of management time;
- the cost of hiring or training replacement staff;
- loss of business, either short term or long term;
- legal costs.

Even for the items covered by insurance, over time, premiums will increase to reflect the claims record of the organization, just as happens to a private car driver with a poor accident record.

The more far-sighted organizations now look at losses due to breaches of security just like any other business cost, and include them amongst the factors by which they judge managers' performance levels. Some will not insure some aspects of their activities where there is no legal requirement to do so. Instead, they require managers to control the costs of security just like raw material costs, fuel costs or commission to sales staff.

The moral and legal dimensions

Insurance does not deal with the moral obligations to protect staff, customers and visitors from harm, increasingly backed by the threat of legal action which can lead to substantial fines or even imprisonment. Those which will **not** be insurable risks.

Company property

Some employees believe that theft of company or organization's property – or damage to it – doesn't matter as the costs are borne by the management or some impersonal organization which has infinite amounts of money.

But no organization is prepared to keep replacing assets that are stolen or wrecked by misuse. There is always another option, which could involve buying in materials from elsewhere, or ultimately the closure of a site that is proving too costly to run. This has happened to retail stores where more stock was apparently leaving via the staff exit than through the checkouts.

It is also over optimistic, to say the least, to believe that dishonest people will distinguish between the cash and property of individuals and that of the organization. It may be taboo to 'shop' people known to be pilfering goods or money from the organization, but, there is a real risk that staff who will not help catch them will find themselves the victim of crime, or reckless behaviour.

The mistaken belief that theft or abuse of the organization's property is not important is one that you should address regularly when talking to your team members. Remind them that there are direct and indirect risks to their personal prosperity and that it is not in any of their interests for the organization to fail.

3.5 Malicious attack

It is a regrettable fact that violence at work has increased in recent years. The figures vary from one workplace to another, with some much more prone than others.

Activity 25

> Around 20% of UK employees have been physically threatened whilst at work. In other countries, the figures are much worse. In the USA, the most frequent cause of death for female employees is murder.

This list includes five of the workplaces that have the worst records for violence at work. Which do you think they are? Underline five.

1   Petrol retailers

2   Hotels and guest houses

3   DHSS benefits offices

4   Pubs

5   Nightclubs

6   Shopping centres

7   Hospitals

8   Sports centres

9   Restaurants

The answers to this activity may or may not surprise you, depending on where you work and spend your leisure time. The following five workplaces have the worst record for violence at work:

■   petrol retailers;
■   DHSS benefits offices;

- pubs;
- nightclubs;
- hospitals.

The one ambiguous category is probably shopping centres. As a whole, they are not the riskiest places, but many individual outlets are right at the top of the list, whether in shopping centres or on high streets, especially those selling:

- alcohol;
- jewellery;
- electrical goods, which are of high value, portable and have a ready market through illegal outlets of various kinds.

Analyses of assaults on employees at work show that around 40% of assaults are by customers, 25% by outsiders, including criminals, and 20% by colleagues.

Who are the attackers?

Customers or users of services in places, such as hospital accident and emergency wards, are by far the most frequent offenders. Outsiders generally are the next most frequent assailants, with work colleagues the least likely attackers.

4 Using the five-step approach to risk assessment

Now that we have looked in detail at a variety of security risks, we will look at the five-step approach to risk assessment more closely, by applying it to the problem of malicious attack.

How prone your organization is to attack will depend on what you do and where you do it. You need to do a proper risk assessment following the five-step approach.

1   **Identify** the resources at risk. In this case, you know that the resource at risk is the human one.

2   **Assess** the **probability** that the risk will be realized. This will depend on the circumstances, e.g. employees most probably at risk are those who:

- work alone and/or at nights, perhaps making security checks;
- work on remote sites;
- transport valuable merchandise;
- handle or transport cash at any stage;
- visit customers at home for any reason – especially if alone;
- deal with members of the general public who may be influenced by alcohol.

3   **Evaluate** the consequences. These could include serious injury or death.

4   **Prioritize** the consequences. You will need to look at which employee, or category of employees, is most at risk. Take account of all the evidence that exists for the field you work in, from similar organizations, trade bodies and government sources.

5   **Implement** a strategy to eliminate or minimize the risks, tackling the worst first. Remember that all individuals or groups at risk of serious injury must be given equal top priority.

Implementing a strategy for risk reduction

Now, follow through the fifth step in detail: Implement a strategy to eliminate or minimize the risk, with **elimination** being the real aim where people are at risk.

As an example, look at the situation where an employee visits customers at home. Many employees do, including estate agents, meter readers, sales personnel, service engineers, social services personnel and nurses.

A checklist approach

A simple checklist will help you to clarify the issues.

1   Is there another way of doing the job? If YES then IMPLEMENT IT and so eliminate the risk. If NO then continue through checklist.

2   Should some areas be declared 'out of bounds' for home visits? This decision can be based on previous experience and records.

3   Should some categories of people be refused home visits? This can be based on records/profiles of likely offenders.

4   Should we provide a second person as back up?

5   Have we provided suitable training for staff? Such training should include how to recognize and deal with signs of potential violence.

6   Do we have systems and equipment for checking where staff are and that they are safe at pre-determined intervals? Are they enforced at all times, including outside office hours?

7   Is suitable protective equipment required and is it available? Are staff trained to use it?

8   Have we sufficient expertise to create a secure system for ourselves? Should we consult outside experts?

Security issues are frequently complex and involve sensitive matters, especially where there could be a danger of injury to employees or even loss of life. Using the five-step approach followed by the checklist to develop your strategy will help you to ensure that important issues are not forgotten.

In this case, we considered the risk to people, but the same approach works for equipment, stock and data.

4.1 The costs of security

Security measures can be extremely expensive to implement. Eventually, the **cost** of achieving security may **equal or outweigh** the **value** of the resources being protected.

As this point approaches, organizations must ask themselves if each succeeding increase in cost is justifiable, or whether perhaps the activity is not viable and affordable.

Eurotunnel spent millions of pounds trying to protect Calais terminal from ingress by inmates of the nearby Sangatte refugee camp. On many occasions, trains were halted, or the whole operation paralysed for substantial periods. This security issue threatened the viability of an entire international transport operation with Europe-wide implications for rail and road traffic.

Where people's lives are at risk, the issues become very complex and in general terms it is not legally or morally acceptable to say 'we'd like to improve their security, but we can't afford to'. In such circumstances, the eventual decision may be to eliminate the activity associated with the risk altogether, for example:

- by closing a restaurant **before** a local pub turns out customers who have a record of violent and offensive behaviour;
- by eliminating payment of wages in cash and persuading all employees to accept payment by bank transfer;
- by ceasing to stock lines that are constantly being stolen, or moving them to counter service rather than self service situations.

Security issues are seldom simple to manage. Elimination is not an option for the accident and emergency facility in an inner city hospital, at least not in this country, with its long and proud tradition of caring for the sick or injured, so, the only option is to **minimize the risks** and ensure that the people who face them are trained and equipped to face it.

4.2 Security policy

EXTENSION 5
This is a model security policy for you to compare with existing security policies.

While the most important factor in achieving security is the attitude and behaviour of employees at every level, it is good practice for all organizations to have a formal security policy.

Activity 26

15 mins

Look through the model security policy in extension 5.

1   If your organization already has a policy, compare it with the model. Are there differences? If there are, should your organization consider making any changes? Provide a one page summary of the differences you notice.

2   If your organization does not have a policy, consider if you should recommend introducing one to appropriate managers within your organization. Produce a draft based on the model.

Self-assessment 3

15 mins

1   What do you understand by the concept of vulnerability and how does it differ from hazard in risk assessments for safety?

   _____

   _____

2   a For many organizations, the worst security nightmare nowadays is the
      _____ or malicious _____ of _____
      _____

   b Professional _____ _____ approaches are the best means of assuring the security of _____ _____
      _____ and _____

   c Why is it important for an organization to have a written security policy, made known to all employees?

   d Using the 'what if' question is a simple but effective way of _____
      _____ of a risk minimization strategy.

   e Customers and users of services account for _____ per cent of malicious attacks on _____.

Answers to these questions are on page 80.

5 Summary

- Security management should flow from a clear statement of policy, backed with appropriate resources and proper organization and arrangements, including training at all levels and the clear indication that disciplinary action will be taken against any employee who breaches the policy.

- Risk assessments and frequent use of the 'what if' question are essential elements of professional security management. The potential consequences of identified risks must be dealt with on the basis of tackling the 'worst first'.

- Professional risk management will deter most potential offenders and save time in any investigations.

- The most important single aspect of security is the attitude of managers, who must set the right example to employees, contractors and customers at all times.

- Restricting access to stock and sensitive areas and disseminating information on the 'need to know' principle are important aspects of a security policy.

- Careless talk in an organizational security context can cost livelihoods.

- Complete security is an unachievable goal for any organization – the cost would outweigh the value of the savings achieved.

Performance checks

■ 1 Quick quiz

Jot down the answers to the following questions on *Managing the Effective Use of Equipment.*

Question 1   Explain, in your own words, the purpose of method study.

_____

_____

_____

_____

_____

Question 2   List the **six** steps of method study.

_____

_____

_____

_____

_____

_____

Question 3   What methods of recording can be used during the recording stage of method study?

_____

_____

Question 4   What, in brief, is a string diagram used for?

_____

_____

Question 5   Give a definition of work measurement.

_____

_____

Question 6   What is continuous improvement and why is it an effective means of embed-ding change?

_____

_____

Question 7   What aspects of work can be affected by staff changes?

_____

Question 8   List three costs that a team leader needs to know and understand in relation to the use of resources.

_____

_____

_____

Question 9   What do you understand by the 'need to know' principle?

_____

_____

_____

Question 10   It is not legally or morally acceptable to reject expensive security measures when the _____ and_____ of people are involved.

Question 11   What are the limitations of a 'restricted access' policy?

_____

_____

_____

Answers to these questions can be found on pages 82–3.

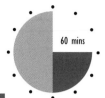

 ## 2 Workbook assessment

Read the following case incident, and then deal with the questions which follow. Write your answers on a separate sheet of paper.

> The management of the Sawbridge Timber and Frame Company would like to improve efficiency in the loading and transport of timber.
>
> Jason White, one of their managers, is assigned to carry out an investigation of the problems in this area, and to propose a way forward. He is given authority to recommend any steps he believes are necessary, provided he is able to justify the expense.
>
> After conducting a preliminary survey, Jason notes down two points as being the main problems resulting in inefficiency.
>
> (a) Lorries are loaded by fork-lift truck. The process is slow, and there have been a number of incidents in which timber was damaged while being loaded. In one case, the cab of a lorry was crushed by falling timber, the driver fortunately not being in the cab at the time.
> (b) During transport, average journey times seem to be longer than Jason would have expected.

In answering the following questions, you do not need to write more than a total of a page or so.

1 Suggest **four** possible reasons for the apparent slow and poor handling of timber during the loading process.

2 Assume that, in turn, each one of the four possible reasons listed in (1) is the actual problem. Explain briefly your ideas for finding a solution to this problem.

3 Suggest **three** possible reasons for the long journey times during transport.

4 Assume that, in turn, each one of the three possible reasons listed in question 3 is the actual problem. Briefly describe your ideas on potential solutions, setting out associated costs and benefits where possible.

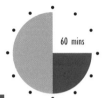

S/NVQ
D6

3 Work-based assignment

The time guide for this assignment gives you an approximate idea of how long it is likely to take you to write up your findings. You will find you need to spend some additional time gathering information, talking to colleagues, and thinking about the assignment.

Your written response to this assignment may provide the basis of appropriate evidence for your S/NVQ portfolio.

What you have to do

In Session B, you should have begun work on a number of Activities designed to help you plan for the increased efficiency of your work team and work area. The relevant activities were:

People: Activity 8 on page 27, and 14 on page 34.

Workspace: Activity 9 on page 28, and 15 on page 35.

Equipment: Activity 10 on page 29, and 16 on page 36.

Materials: Activity 11 on page 30, and 17 on page 37.

Information: Activity 13 on page 32, and 19 on page 40.

Select one of the five resource items. Develop a plan to put in place changes that will result in demonstrable improvement in efficiency and effectiveness of work processes in your work area. This might include suggestions on potential areas of waste reduction, purchase or update of equipment, enhancing the skills and knowledge of staff.

Present your work in the form of a report addressed to your manager and any other individuals who will be part of the decision-making process if any of your changes are implemented. The content of the report should include:

■ resource area selected, with reasons for your selection
■ an account of the work you carried out during your investigations
■ cost benefit analysis
■ illustrations of the methods and techniques employed, for example the waste reduction six-stage process.

Reflect and review

1 Reflect and review

Now that you have completed your work on *Managing the Effective Use of Equipment*, let us review our workbook objectives.

■ You will be better able to identify and use some method study techniques to help you improve efficiency and effectiveness.

You may not want to claim that you have become a method study expert as a result of reading this workbook, but you should have a better understanding of the techniques which might be available to you. All of these require the full commitment of higher management, and you would no doubt need to obtain approval before introducing any of them in your area.

■ Which of the techniques described in Session A do you feel would be useful in your work situation?

_____

_____

_____

■ How might you go about investigating the subject further?

_____

_____

_____

■ You will be better able to plan for the best use of resources assigned to you.

We spent a lot of time discussing resources. The Activities you tackled in Session B should have helped you to make plans to use the resources you have more efficiently.

As you should already have made some effort at developing resource plans, you might like now to consider the following two questions.

■ Are my resources adequate for my team's needs?

_____

_____

_____

■ What new approaches to resource efficiency can I think of?

_____

_____

_____

■ You will be better able to contribute effectively to the control of your organization's resources.

Efficiency involves controlling resources as well as planning for their best use. By reducing materials waste, for example, or using equipment to its full potential, you are controlling them, and saving your organization money in doing so.

■ Which types of resource do I feel I do **not** have under adequate control?

_____

_____

_____

■ What kinds of extra controls could I introduce to limit the wastage of resources?

_____

_____

_____

■ You will be better able to play your part in helping to improve the efficiency of your work team and your organization.

This is the main purpose of the workbook, and all your efforts have been directed towards this aim.

■ What extra contribution might I make to the efficiency of my work team and/or my organization?

_____

_____

_____

■ How might I go about persuading my colleagues of the benefits of planning for improved efficiency?

_____

_____

_____

■ You will be better able to identify risks to physical, human and information resources and have gained some practical ideas and experience with which to guard against them.

All managers have a responsibility for the security of the resources which they manage, including the 'human' resources. You have had opportunity to look at a number of aspects of this vast subject, which perplexes not only commercial organizations but governments throughout the world, including the following.

■ The varied nature of security risks and their repercussions.
■ The five-step risk management approach to security management and the use of 'what if' questions to help you plan for contingencies.
■ The need to balance security considerations against the safety rights of people who need to escape rapidly from buildings.
■ The need to apply 'common sense' strategies to prevent opportunist or audacious attempts to breach security.
■ The restriction of access to premises, stocks and information to protect security.
■ The mistake in believing that insurance means that losses 'don't matter' or that losses don't matter because 'it's only company property'.
■ The increasing need to guard against malicious attacks on personnel.
■ The costs v. savings balance and the threat of business closure when costs of security become unsustainable.
■ The need for a security policy published to and applicable to personnel at all levels, backed up by the example which managers set to their staff at all times.

What specific messages will you take from this session and apply to make your own work area secure, or recommend for use more widely within your organization?

_____

_____

_____

_____

▪ 2 Action plan

Use this plan to further develop for yourself a course of action you want to take. Make a note in the left-hand column of the issues or problems you want to tackle, and then decide what you intend to do, and make a note in column 2.

The resources you need might include time, materials, information or money. You may need to negotiate for some of them, but they could be something easily acquired, like half an hour of somebody's time, or a chapter of a book. Put whatever you need in column 3. No plan means anything without a timescale, so put a realistic target completion date in column 4.

Finally, describe the outcome you want to achieve as a result of this plan, whether it is for your own benefit or advancement, or a more efficient way of doing things.

Desired outcomes

Issues	2 Action	3 Resources	4 Target completion

Actual outcomes

3 Extensions

Extension 1

Book   *Operations Management*
Author   Howard Barnett
Edition   Second edition, 1996
Publisher Palgrave Macmillan
ISBN   0 3336 6210 5

Operations Management provides a comprehensive introduction, clearly written and jargon-free, concentrating on examining the ways an organization turns its resources into goods or services. Some relevant chapters are Planning and Control, Managing the Costs, Managing the Processes, Managing Performance I: Getting the Methods Right, Managing Performance 2: Measuring Work Content, Managing Performance: Incentive Schemes, Managing Time and Managing Numbers 2: Statistical Process Control.

Extension 2

Book   *Introduction to Operations Management*
Author   John Naylor
Edition   2002
Publisher Prentice Hall
ISBN   0 2736 5578 7

This book covers a number of the subjects of this workbook, including efficiency and effectiveness, transformation processes, work study, benchmarking, Total Quality Management, and continuous improvement. Particular chapters relevant to our subject are: Chapter 6 – Studying work; Chapter 8 – Facility layout: manufacture and isolated service; Chapter 9 – Facility layout: personal and self service.

As the Preface says: 'This book gives a comprehensive coverage of operations management for those who come to the subject for the first time.'

Extension 3

Book   *Essentials of Production and Operations Management*
Author   Ray Wild
Edition   Fifth edition, 2001
Publisher The Continuum International Publishing Group
ISBN   0 8264 5254 X

This book covers all aspects of the operations and production management function, with a number of useful case studies to show how it inter-relates to the purchasing, supply, logistics and materials handling functions, in the use of systems like JIT, MRP and automated handling.

Extension 4

FIVE-STEP APPROACH TO ASSESSING AND MINIMIZING SECURITY RISKS				
Brief description of situation				
RESOURCES AFFECTED				
	HUMAN	STOCK	EQUIPMENT	DATA
1 Identify resources at risk				
2 Probability that risk will be realized				
3 Evaluate consequences				
4 Prioritize consequences				
5 Recommended strategy to eliminate or minimize the risks (tackling the 'worst first')				

MODEL SECURITY POLICY

POLICY STATEMENT

It is the Policy of the _____ organization to assure the security of its human, physical and information resources against harm or abuse, however arising.

This Policy will apply to _____ property and that of all employees whilst on company premises, provided that they have complied with the security procedures for their areas.

RESOURCES

The Chief Executive is responsible for ensuring that a level of resources is provided to eliminate or minimize each risk assessed commensurate with the consequences of the risks identified.

RESPONSIBILITIES

Board Level

Overall responsibility for implementing this Policy rests with the _____ Executive.

Management Level

All Managers are required to take responsibility for their defined areas of operation.

All employees

Are required to act at all times with respect towards the property of the organization, colleagues and all other people with whom they have dealings.

They must obey all reasonable instructions regarding security, including those concerning searches of vehicles, lockers and the person in accordance with the procedures agreed with staff representatives.

Employees and Managers at any level who flout security procedures, deliberately or recklessly, will be subject to disciplinary procedures which may lead to dismissal.

RISK ASSESSMENT

This organization will require all Managers to conduct formal Risk Assessments for their areas of responsibility, using the standard Organization system in its current edition.

Managers will be required to assign priorities to the risks identified for their areas.

- To deal directly with those for which they have adequate resources available.
- To make recommendations and requests for assistance for resources for identified risks which they cannot deal with directly.

TRAINING & SUPERVISION

The Organization will provide appropriate training and supervision identified as necessary by the risk assessments provided:

- including training in the implementation of all matters relating to the implementation of this Policy.

PUBLISHING AND UPDATING

The _____ Executive will be responsible for:

- publishing this policy throughout the organization;
- updating it whenever necessary to keep it in accord with any legislation affecting it and with 'best practices' for this aspect of management.

SIGNED _____ **Chief Executive**

DATED _____ **2** _____ **EDITION No.** _____

These extensions can be taken up via your ILM Centre. They will either have them or will arrange that you have access to them. However, it may be more convenient to check out the materials with your personnel or training people at work – they may well give you access. There are other good reasons for approaching your own people; for example, they will become aware of your interest and you can involve them in your development.

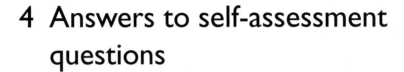

4 Answers to self-assessment questions

**Self-assessment 1
on pages 20–1**

1   The overall productivity is:

$$\frac{\text{output}}{\text{input}} = \frac{4500}{2500} = 1.8$$

The output per head is:

$$\frac{£4500}{5} = £900$$

2   (a) QUANTITATIVE is the term used when costs are described in numerical terms or units. QUALITATIVE is the term used when costs are set out in broad descriptive or less tangible terms.

(b) To justify the purchase of a new piece of equipment, or any form of change, it is generally accepted that the total BENEFITS will exceed the total costs.

(c) In undertaking any form of WORK MEASUREMENT the business will be seeking to identify and introduce methods for improving process efficiency.

(d) In the second stage of time study you will break down the job into phases called ELEMENTS.

3   The correct diagram is:

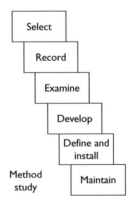

4   The four main areas of consideration in method study are financial, technical, human and environmental.

5   Factors that affect managers in their own working area in relation to human resource planning include:

- numbers of staff needed to carry out current work requirements
- skills and knowledge levels required to carry out these work requirements, possibly in the form of job specifications for each role within the department or team
- potential changes to work requirements, based on information gathered
- organizational, departmental and team objectives
- number and types of staff required to fulfil these objectives.

Self-assessment 2 on pages 40–1

1   (a) If you get your team fully MOTIVATED and working towards the right OBJECTIVES, efficiency and effectiveness will follow almost automatically.
    (b) A COACH is someone who aims to get the best out of people: the best EFFORTS, the best ACHIEVEMENTS, the best IDEAS.
    (c) It is the TEAM who must get the job done, and it is the LEADER's role to provide them with the means to do it: to EMPOWER them.
    (d) Badly used workspace can result in CONGESTION, ACCIDENTS, inefficient COMMUNICATIONS, excessive ENERGY costs or low PRODUCTION.

2   Ways to save energy in an office could include:

- switching off lights and heating when they aren't needed
- switching off equipment when it isn't needed
- keeping doors and windows closed when heating is on
- getting the building properly insulated.

3   Some suggestions are:

- keep better records of expenditure, ensuring they are complete, accurate and accessible
- ensure you monitor and maintain resources such as equipment and materials in accordance with organizational requirements
- keep your team members informed of their individual responsibilities for the control of resources.

4   Examples of costs associated with the use of resources include:

- costs of running an item of equipment
- costs of an item of equipment lying idle
- cost of running a faulty, poorly maintained item of equipment
- costs of staff
- costs of replacing staff
- costs of producing items, and the marginal costs of producing just one more item than is required.

Self-assessment 3 on page 63

1   'Vulnerability' is the intrinsic attraction of a resource to a potential thief. It differs from 'hazard' in that it is almost always impossible to eliminate it in the way that you often can a hazard. Without the 'vulnerability' of items like alcohol, diamonds or electrical goods, there would be no business.

2   a   For many organizations, the worst security nightmare nowadays is the THEFT or malicious CORRUPTION of ELECTRONIC DATA.

    b   Professional RISK MANAGEMENT approaches are the best means of assuring the security of PERSONNEL STOCK EQUIPMENT and DATA.

    c   Having a written Security Policy, made known to all employees, shows everyone that the organization takes the subject seriously; cares about what happens to employees and their property and that resources will be committed to assuring security based on proper risk assessment.

    d   Using the 'what if' question is a simple but effective way of VERIFYING THE EFFECTIVENESS of a risk minimization strategy.

    e   Customers and users of services account for 40 per cent of malicious attacks on PERSONNEL.

5 Answers to activities

Activity 2 on page 6

The costs can be classified as follows:

1   In the investigation of possible suppliers, calls are **quantitative**, travel is **quantitative**, time is **qualitative**.

2   The actual purchase (or lease if this is an option) is **quantitative**.

3   The installation and commissioning of the equipment is **quantitative**.

4   The delivery and location on-site is **quantitative** and **qualitative**.

5   Time spent training staff on how to use is **quantitative** and **qualitative**.

6   Running of existing equipment during phasing-in stage – duplicate costs are **quantitative**.

7   In regard to down time if old equipment is to be removed before installation of new, loss of profit is **quantitative**, loss of time is **qualitative**.

8   Staff down time while waiting for installation loss of profit is **quantitative**, loss of time is **qualitative**.

9   The potential opportunity costs are both all the **quantitative** costs listed above and all the **qualitative** costs, plus any other relevant factors.

Activity 22
on page 50

FIVE-STEP APPROACH TO ASSESING AND MINIMIZING SECURITY RISKS				
Brief description of situation: Extension to a cash and carry warehouse During the three-month project, up to 20 contractors' staff will be working on site and will have to gain access via the main staff entrance and existing warehouse. Some overhead work will be involved and at some stage, the contractors will need to break through the existing external wall, close to some high storage racking. The main computer terminal will have to be moved to a new office. It has been agreed that contractors staff can use company fork lift trucks, provided that they are licensed drivers and obtain formal permission from you on every occasion. Of the 50 company staff on site, around 40 are paid in cash on Thursday afternoons.				
RESOURCES AFFECTED				
	HUMAN	STOCK & CASH	EQUIPMENT	DATA
I Identify resources at risk	Employees, contractors' staff and customers	Stock and cash from tills and payroll	Racking and fork lift trucks Computer terminal	Data stored in computer
2 Probability that risk will be realized	Medium to high	Medium to high	Medium	Medium
3 Evaluate consequences	Serious injury or death in 'worst case' scenario	Substantial loss of stock and cash	Serious damage to trucks, buildings, racking and terminal	Serious loss of sensitive data
4 Prioritize consequences	**(1)** **worst**	**(2)** **second worst**	**(3)** **third worst**	**(4)** **fourth worst**
5 Recommended strategy to eliminate or minimize the risks (tackling the 'worst first')	**(1)** Agree safety plan with contractors. Agree supervisory arrangements and site liaison for contractors and their employees or sub-contractors. Check and upgrade first aid arrangements as necessary. **(2)** Demand verification of contractors' staff backgrounds. Agree search procedures for contractors' vehicles and personnel. Upgrade security checks for stock and cash. Impose 'unbreakable rules' for access to site and 'signing in and out' of contractors' employees, identified by badges/lapel badges with photographs etc. **(3)** Agree strict 'ground rules' for checking fork lift truck licenses; identification of holders (e.g. lapel badges). Clear procedures regarding the misuse of equipment, including summary dismissal from site. **(4)** Schedule computer move at best (quietest) moment available. Check on electrical works. Ensure back up systems working and constantly up-to-date.				

⬤ 6 Answers to the quick quiz

Answer 1   Method study can be defined as: 'Systematically recording the way work is done, followed by analysis and development of the new methods, with the aim of doing the work better.'

Answer 2   We listed the steps of method study as: select, record, examine, develop, define and install, and maintain.

Answer 3   The recording methods that can be used are flow process diagrams, string diagrams and multiple activity charts.

Answer 4   A string diagram is used to determine the distance travelled by a person (or materials, equipment or information).

Answer 5   Work measurement is defined as the use of techniques to establish how long it takes a qualified worker to do a specified job to a defined level of performance.

Answer 6   In continuous improvement staff make suggestions on potential improvements that can be made. Continuous improvement is recognized as a more effective means of embedding change where suggestions for improvement have been made by those who are most affected by this change.

Answer 7   The aspects of work affected by staff changes are productivity and quality.

Answer 8   Costs that a manager needs to know and understand in relation to the use of resources include:

   ■ the costs to running an item of equipment
   ■ the costs of an item of equipment lying idle
   ■ the costs of running a faulty, poorly maintained item of equipment
   ■ the costs of staff
   ■ the costs of replacing staff
   ■ the costs of producing items, and the marginal costs of producing just one more item than is required.

Answer 9   That information is not given to people who will not have to use it in the work which they do. The principle should be applied throughout the 'hierarchy' of an organization to protect confidential information which might fall into the hands of a competitor.

Answer 10   It is not legally or morally acceptable to reject expensive security measures when the LIVES and LIMBS of people are involved.

Answer 11   There are many sites to which large numbers of members of the general public and employees have to have general access, making it difficult to keep them away from any but the most sensitive areas. Even without that constraint, such a policy is still only as good as the people who work in the areas, who must unfailingly challenge 'strangers' or people not having the correct identification, however important they may look.

7 Certificate

Completion of this certificate by an authorized person shows that you have worked through all the parts of this workbook and satisfactorily completed the assessments. The certificate provides a record of what you have done that may be used for exemptions or as evidence of prior learning against other nationally certificated qualifications.

superseries

Managing the Effective Use of Equipment

....

has satisfactorily completed this workbook

Name of signatory ....

Position ....

Signature ....

Date ....

Official stamp

Pergamon
Flexible
Learning

Fifth Edition

superseries

FIFTH EDITION

Workbooks in the series:

Achieving Objectives Through Time Management	978-0-08-046415-2
Building the Team	978-0-08-046412-1
Coaching and Training your Work Team	978-0-08-046418-3
Communicating One-to-One at Work	978-0-08-046438-1
Developing Yourself and Others	978-0-08-046414-5
Effective Meetings for Managers	978-0-08-046439-8
Giving Briefings and Making Presentations in the Workplace	978-0-08-046436-7
Influencing Others at Work	978-0-08-046435-0
Introduction to Leadership	978-0-08-046411-4
Managing Conflict in the Workplace	978-0-08-046416-9
Managing Creativity and Innovation in the Workplace	978-0-08-046441-1
Managing Customer Service	978-0-08-046419-0
Managing Health and Safety at Work	978-0-08-046426-8
Managing Performance	978-0-08-046429-9
Managing Projects	978-0-08-046425-1
Managing Stress in the Workplace	978-0-08-046417-6
Managing the Effective Use of Equipment	978-0-08-046432-9
Managing the Efficient Use of Materials	978-0-08-046431-2
Managing the Employment Relationship	978-0-08-046443-5
Marketing for Managers	978-0-08-046974-4
Motivating to Perform in the Workplace	978-0-08-046413-8
Obtaining Information for Effective Management	978-0-08-046434-3
Organizing and Delegating	978-0-08-046422-0
Planning Change in the Workplace	978-0-08-046444-2
Planning to Work Efficiently	978-0-08-046421-3
Providing Quality to Customers	978-0-08-046420-6
Recruiting, Selecting and Inducting New Staff in the Workplace	978-0-08-046442-8
Solving Problems and Making Decisions	978-0-08-046423-7
Understanding Change in the Workplace	978-0-08-046424-4
Understanding Culture and Ethics in Organizations	978-0-08-046428-2
Understanding Organizations in their Context	978-0-08-046427-5
Understanding the Communication Process in the Workplace	978-0-08-046433-6
Understanding Workplace Information Systems	978-0-08-046440-4
Working with Costs and Budgets	978-0-08-046430-5
Writing for Business	978-0-08-046437-4

For prices and availability please telephone our order helpline
or email

+44 (0) 1865 474010
directorders@elsevier.com